Cooking School

CHINESE

Cooking School

CHINESE

Bring the flavours of China to life in your own kitchen!

This edition published in 2011
LOVE FOOD is an imprint of Parragon Books Ltd

Parragon
Queen Street House
4 Queen Street
Bath BA1 1HE, UK

www.parragon.com

ISBN: 978-1-4454-7025-2

Printed in China

Internal design by Pink Creative

Notes for the Reader

This book uses both metric and imperial measurements. Follow the same units of measurement throughout; do not mix metric and imperial. All spoon measurements are level: teaspoons are assumed to be 5 ml, and tablespoons are assumed to be 15 ml. Unless otherwise stated, milk is assumed to be full fat, eggs and individual vegetables are medium, and pepper is freshly ground black pepper.

The times given are an approximate guide only. Preparation times differ according to the techniques used by different people and the cooking times may also vary from those given. Optional ingredients, variations or serving suggestions have not been included in the calculations.

Recipes using raw or very lightly cooked eggs should be avoided by infants, the elderly, pregnant women, convalescents and anyone suffering from an illness. Pregnant and breastfeeding women are advised to avoid eating peanuts and peanut products. Sufferers from nut allergies should be aware that some of the ready-made ingredients used in the recipes in this book may contain nuts. Always check the packaging before use.

Contents

Introduction

Mastering the basics of Chinese cooking will give you a marvellous opportunity not only to explore the fabulous array of ingredients, the all-important preparation techniques and the different cooking methods, but also to go deeper into the history, geography and culture that lie behind Chinese regional cuisines. Armed with this knowledge, you will be amazed at the ease with which you can create an impressive range of dishes in your own kitchen, whether for a multi-dish Chinese meal or as a simple accompaniment to your normal menu.

Regional Cooking

China is as vast as the United States, spanning many degrees of latitude. It has radical variations in climate ranging from year-round sub-arctic conditions in the north, to sweltering tropical heat in the southern coastal regions. China's topography is equally extreme. From the Tibetan Plateau in the north-west (3,600 m/11,800 ft) the land descends in a series of steps to the fertile coastal plains in the east and south. It is this diversity of topography and climate that lies behind the intriguing variations of regional cooking.

Beijing (northern cuisine)

The food in this region relies on staples such as wheat, sorghum, millet and soya beans. Wheat is a major crop, which means that that noodles, rather than rice, are the order of the day. The food tends to be homely and robust, though the well-known Peking Duck is an exception. Hearty lamb dishes are popular, such as Lamb with Black Bean Sauce, reflecting the influence of Chinese Muslims who, for religious reasons, eat lamb rather than pork.

Canton (southern cuisine)

Cantonese cuisine offers an astonishing array of culinary feasts and is renowned for top-notch seafood, fresh fruit and vegetables, stunning stir-fries and dim sum to die for. Considered the gold standard of Chinese cuisine, Cantonese food is the best known in the Western world, thanks to large numbers of Chinese who emigrated to Europe and the United States in the nineteenth century. Cantonese dishes, such as Sweet and Sour Pork, and Sweet and Sour Spare Ribs, are well known the world over.

Since Canton was the first Chinese trading port, the region is hugely influenced by foreign contact. For example, broccoli and asparagus were introduced from abroad and were popular in Canton before being taken up elsewhere. Cooking with fruit and fruit-based sauces, as in Fruity Duck Stir-fry, is also typical of the region. Seasonings are typically kept light, with limited use of soy sauce, in order to let the ingredients shine.

Shanghai (eastern cuisine)

Based around the Yangtze delta, this fertile region produces both rice and wheat as well as an abundance of fruit and vegetables. Fresh fish comes not only from the sea but also from the numerous lakes and rivers that criss-cross the land. Perhaps least known in the West, Shanghai cuisine is a mixture of styles, characterized by rich complex flavours and the lavish use of the rich soy sauce for which the Yangtze delta is renowned. Sugar is also a key ingredient, especially in salty dishes in which it balances flavour without introducing obvious sweetness.

Szechuan (western cuisine)

Known in China as 'the land of plenty', Szechuan enjoys rich fertile soil, a warm climate and copious rainfall. The region produces an enormous variety of fruit, vegetables, fungi and fish, which are put to good use in richly flavoured, heavily sauced dishes.

Szechuanese cuisine has much more to offer than the hot and spicy dishes for which it is famous in the West. Though chillies and pepper are certainly used as 'warming' foods to counteract the region's inherent dampness, these pungent seasonings are never allowed to overwhelm other ingredients. Delicately flavoured bamboo shoots and tofu feature in the cuisine, and in restaurants 'cool' and 'medium' dishes as well as 'hot' are usually on the menu. The region is also noted for pickled or dry-salted vegetables.

Cooking and Eating Styles

For the Chinese, food and its supply have always been of vital concern; food is deeply appreciated and nothing is ever wasted. Regardless of region, it is is prepared, cooked and served in accordance with the age-old Taoist principles of Yin and Yang in which balance and contrast are key. Some of the ingredients and cooking methods may vary from one region to another, but basically all dishes are unmistakably 'Chinese'.

What distinguishes Chinese food is the emphasis on the harmonious blending of colour, texture, aroma and flavour, both in a single dish and in the dishes that make up the meal. Of great importance is 'fire control' as the Chinese call it; there are at least forty different methods of heating food! Understanding the basics, such as preheating a wok until almost red-hot, will help you to achieve the necessary texture, whether it be crisp or soft, wet or dry, slippery or crunchy.

Timing is equally important. If the heat is sufficiently high, food will cook very quickly, but beginners tend to make the mistake of cooking food for too long over too low a heat.

Also important are the size and the shape of the prepared ingredient, which must be appropriate for a particular method of cooking. For example, food for quick stir-frying is cut into small thin slices of uniform size, and never into large chunks. This is not only for appearance's sake, but also because ingredients of the same size and shape cook in the same amount of time.

Chinese meals and snacks

Day-to-day meals eaten at home are usually fairly simple though made up of a variety of dishes. The meal is served all at once, in contrast to a formal banquet where dishes are served in a prescribed sequence. Unlike Western convention, dishes are never allocated to individual diners; everything on the table is shared. The Chinese do not usually finish a meal with a dessert, although sweet dishes might punctuate a full-scale banquet and fruit might be served at the end of a multi-course restaurant meal. Sweet dishes are usually eaten between meals as snacks.

Snacking and street food play a big part in Chinese culture. The Chinese love to buy all manner of tasty snacks freshly cooked at roadside stalls, eating them on the hoof as they go about their daily life. In the evening, the pavements are filled with groups of families and friends cooking, selling and sharing delicious food. Living in overcrowded conditions as many Chinese do, getting together in this way is an important and enjoyable part of social life.

Menu Planning

For a shared meal allow one dish per person. For example, if cooking for only two or three people, serve one main dish with a vegetable side dish and a rice or noodle dish, plus a soup if you like. For an informal meal for four to six people, serve four dishes plus soup and rice; for a formal dinner for the same number allow six to eight dishes. When cooking for large numbers always increase the number of dishes rather than the quantity of ingredients. That way, you'll have more variety of flavour, colour and texture.

Fundamental Techniques

Chopping

Cut the ingredients into small evenly sized pieces so that they cook in the same amount of time. Shredding vegetables thinly and slicing them diagonally increases the surface area in contact with the hot oil and speeds up cooking.

Stir-frying

Success depends on the wok being very hot before you add the oil – hold your hand flat about 7cm/ 2¾ inches above the base until you feel the heat. Before you begin, have all the ingredients measured and prepared. Using a long-handled ladle or long wooden cooking chopsticks, constantly stir the ingredients so that they all come in contact with the hot oil and are evenly cooked.

Deep-frying

Use enough oil to give a depth of about 5 cm/2 inches. Heat it over a medium–high heat until a faint haze appears. If the oil is not hot enough, the food will act like a sponge and become soggy and greasy. Cook in small batches so as not to overcrowd the pan, which will reduce the temperature and lead to unevenly cooked food. Remove the food with a wire ladle or tongs and drain thoroughly on kitchen paper.

Steaming

Dependent on very fresh ingredients, steaming is routinely used in China to cook a wide range of foods including whole fish, dumplings, vegetables and morsels of poultry and meat. The food is placed on a plate or in a perforated container above boiling liquid in the base of a wok and covered with a lid to trap the steam, which then permeates the food. Depending on size and density, food may be steamed for 10 minutes or up to 3 hours. Ingredients must be very fresh to benefit from this technique.

Braising and red-cooking

Braising is generally used for tougher cuts of meat and dense-fleshed vegetables. The ingredients are briefly stir-fried then simmered in stock until tender. Red-stewing is a similar technique in which food is slowly braised in a rich reddish-brown sauce; soy sauce and sugar are key ingredients. Once cooked, the food takes on the colour of the sauce and becomes meltingly tender.

Cooking Equipment

Chinese cooking tools and utensils have been used for thousands of years and, as such, have proved their worth. Though Western equivalents do an adequate job, a cleaver and a wok will make life easier when you are preparing and cooking Chinese food.

Cleaver

Equally useful for demolishing bones or chopping delicate herbs, the rectangular blade of the cleaver is wide, thick and rigid, before tapering down to a razor-sharp edge. It comes in handy for transferring ingredients from chopping board to wok. Once you become adept, you will be able to use a cleaver to slice, dice, fillet, shred, crush or chop all kinds of food.

Wok

Traditionally made of iron, the wok conducts heat quickly and evenly – essential in Chinese cooking. During stir-frying the conical shape tips the food back to the centre where the heat is most intense. If fitted with a lid and a stand for stability, a wok can also be used for steaming, braising and simmering.

Steamer

The traditional Chinese bamboo steamer has gaps in the bamboo that allow excess moisture to escape, preventing the food from becoming waterlogged. Bamboo steamers come in a range of sizes and can be stacked in a wok or pan of boiling water, allowing you to cook several dishes at the same time.

Ladle

The Chinese use a special ladle for stir-frying. It has a wide shallow bowl that is ideal for lifting, tossing and turning, and an extra-long handle that distances you from the heat. There are also wire mesh ladles that do an efficient job of scooping up deep-fried foods. The wire allows the oil to drain away quickly.

Ingredients

You will need some basic seasonings, oils and storecupboard items, many of which you are likely to have already. Most are easily found in supermarkets, health food shops and Chinese grocers; more obscure items are available by mail order or on-line. The following basics will get you off to a good start.

ALCOHOLS FOR FLAVOURING
Dry sherry or rice wine

NOODLES
Dried egg noodles
Dried rice noodles

NUTS AND SEEDS
Almonds
Cashews
Peanuts
Sesame seeds

OILS
Chilli oil and toasted sesame oil for seasoning
Groundnut oil for stir-frying and deep-frying

RICE
White long-grain

SAUCES
Bean sauce, black and yellow
Chilli bean sauce
Hoisin sauce
Oyster sauce
Plum sauce
Soy sauce: use light soy sauce for stir-fries and dark soy sauce for marinades and red-stewing

SPICES
Cinnamon sticks
Dried chilli flakes
Fennel seeds
Five-spice powder
Ground ginger
Star anise
Szechuan pepper

TOFU (BEAN CURD)
Both firm and soft varieties are useful

VEGETABLES, CANNED OR IN POUCHES
Baby sweetcorn
Bamboo shoots
Lotus root
Salted black beans
Straw mushrooms
Szechuan preserved vegetables
Water chestnuts

VEGETABLES, DRIED
Dried Chinese mushrooms

VINEGARS
White rice vinegar for rice dishes
Brown rice vinegar for marinades and glazes
Black vinegar for slow-cooked stews

Meat and Poultry Dishes

China has countless meat and poultry dishes that are cooked in every imaginable way. Pork is most widely eaten, with poultry coming a close second. Both are versatile, uniformly tender and well suited to Chinese cooking methods. There are fewer beef dishes, partly for economic reasons but also because it is not as versatile – only tender cuts are suitable for stir-frying, and these dry out during slow-cooking. Minced beef is common in Szechuan – Ants Climbing a Tree is a classic dish. Lamb is popular in northern China where religious laws forbid the eating of pork.

Poultry plays an important symbolic role as well as a culinary one. The cock represents positiveness and aggression; the duck, happiness and fidelity; and the pigeon, filial concern and longevity. Turkey

sometimes shows up in Cantonese cooking, but it is not widely eaten in the rest of China because few cooks consider the bird practical and the flesh can sometimes be dry and tough. In China poultry is always purchased live, guaranteeing freshness. Obviously keeping live fowl is not possible – or even desirable – for most Western cooks, but you should buy the best quality you can afford.

Although some classic meat and poultry dishes are found throughout China, many of them vary depending on region. For example, Beef Chop Suey is a Cantonese classic, but Szechuan cooks spike it with pepper and northerners add plenty of garlic. Sweet and Sour Chicken is also typically Cantonese, but Gong Bau Chicken from Szechuan is a complex mix of flavours – hot and spicy as well as sweet and sour.

Wonton Soup

SERVES 6–8

WONTONS

175 g/6 oz minced pork, not too lean

225 g/8 oz raw prawns, peeled, deveined and chopped

½ tsp finely chopped fresh ginger

1 tbsp light soy sauce

1 tbsp Chinese rice wine

2 tsp finely chopped spring onion

pinch of sugar

pinch of white pepper

dash of sesame oil

30 square wonton wrappers

1 egg white, lightly beaten

SOUP

2 litres/3½ pints chicken stock

2 tsp salt

½ tsp white pepper

2 tbsp finely chopped spring onion, to serve

1 tbsp chopped fresh coriander leaves, to serve

1. For the wonton filling, mix together the pork, prawns, ginger, soy sauce, rice wine, spring onion, sugar, pepper and sesame oil and stir well until the texture is thick and pasty. Set aside for at least 20 minutes.

2. To make the wontons, place a teaspoon of the filling at the centre of a wrapper. Brush the edges with a little egg white. Bring the opposite points towards each other and press the edges together, creating a flower-like shape. Repeat with the remaining wrappers and filling.

3. To make the soup, bring the stock to the boil and add the salt and pepper. Boil the wontons in the stock for about 5 minutes, until the wrappers begin to wrinkle around the filling.

4. To serve, put the spring onion in individual bowls, spoon in the wontons and soup and top with the coriander.

Ants Climbing a Tree

SERVES 4–6

55 g/2 oz minced pork
55 g/2 oz minced beef
1 tbsp light soy sauce
pinch of salt
1 tbsp vegetable or groundnut oil
1 tbsp chilli bean paste

1 tsp dark soy sauce
175 ml/6 fl oz hot chicken stock
140 g/5 oz beanthread noodles, soaked in
    warm water for 20 minutes and drained
2 spring onions, finely chopped

1. Combine the minced meats with 1 teaspoon of the light soy sauce and the salt.

2. In a preheated wok or deep saucepan, heat the oil and fry the minced meats until beginning to brown. Add the chilli paste and stir rapidly. Stir in the dark soy sauce.

3. Pour in the stock, noodles and remaining light soy sauce. Cover the wok or pan and simmer for 8–10 minutes, until the pan is quite dry. Shake the pan but do not stir. Toss in the spring onions and serve.

Hoisin Pork with Garlic Noodles

SERVES 4

250 g/9 oz dried thick egg noodles,
  or wholemeal egg noodles
450 g/1 lb pork fillet, thinly sliced
1 tsp sugar
1 tbsp groundnut or corn oil
4 tbsp rice vinegar

4 tbsp white wine vinegar
4 tbsp bottled hoisin sauce
2 spring onions, sliced on the diagonal
about 2 tbsp garlic-flavoured corn oil
2 large garlic cloves, thinly sliced
chopped fresh coriander, to garnish

1. Cook the noodles according to the instructions on the packet. Drain well, rinse under cold water to stop the cooking and drain again, then set aside.

2. Meanwhile, sprinkle the pork slices with the sugar and use your hands to toss together. Heat the oil in a preheated wok or large frying pan. Add the pork and stir-fry for about 3 minutes, until the pork is cooked through and is no longer pink. Use a slotted spoon to remove the pork from the wok and keep warm. Add both vinegars to the wok and boil until they are reduced to about 5 tablespoons. Pour in the hoisin sauce with the spring onions and let it bubble until reduced by half. Add to the pork and stir together.

3. Quickly wipe out the wok and reheat. Add the garlic-flavoured oil and heat until it shimmers. Add the garlic slices and stir round for about 30 seconds, until they are golden and crisp, then use a slotted spoon to scoop them out of the wok and set aside.

4. Add the noodles to the wok and stir them round to warm them through. Divide the noodles between 4 plates, top with the pork and onion mixture and sprinkle over the garlic slices and coriander.

Pork Lo Mein

SERVES 4–6

175 g/6 oz boneless lean pork, shredded

225 g/8 oz dried egg noodles

1½ tbsp vegetable or groundnut oil

2 tsp finely chopped garlic

1 tsp finely chopped fresh ginger

1 carrot, julienned

225 g/8 oz mushrooms, finely sliced

1 green pepper, deseeded and thinly sliced

1 tsp salt

125 ml/4 fl oz hot chicken stock

200 g/7 oz fresh beansprouts, trimmed

2 tbsp finely chopped spring onion

MARINADE

1 tsp light soy sauce

dash of sesame oil

pinch of white pepper

1. Combine all the marinade ingredients in a bowl and marinate the pork for at least 20 minutes.

2. Cook the noodles according to the instructions on the packet. When cooked, drain and set aside.

3. In a preheated wok or deep saucepan, heat 1 teaspoon of the oil and stir-fry the pork until the colour has changed. Remove and set aside.

4. In the clean wok or pan, heat the remaining oil and stir-fry the garlic and ginger until fragrant. Add the carrot and cook for 1 minute, then add the mushrooms and cook for 1 minute. Toss in the pepper and cook for 1 minute. Add the pork, salt and stock and heat through. Finally, toss in the noodles, followed by the beansprouts, and stir well. Sprinkle with the spring onion and serve.

Fried Rice with Pork and Prawns

SERVES 4

1 tbsp vegetable or groundnut oil

1 egg, lightly beaten

100 g/3½ oz raw prawns, peeled, deveined
and cut into 2 pieces

100 g/3½ oz cha siu or smoked bacon,
finely chopped

2 tbsp finely chopped spring onion

200 g/7 oz cooked rice, chilled

1 tsp salt

1. In a preheated wok or deep saucepan, heat 1 teaspoon of the oil and pour in the egg. Cook, stirring, until the egg is lightly set. Remove and set aside.

2. Add the remaining oil and stir-fry the prawns, cha siu and spring onion for about 2 minutes. Add the rice and salt, breaking up the rice into grains, and cook for a further 2 minutes. Finally, stir in the cooked egg. Serve immediately.

Sweet and Sour Pork

SERVES 4

150 ml/5 fl oz vegetable oil, for deep-frying

225 g/8 oz pork fillet, cut into 1-cm/½-inch cubes

1 onion, sliced

1 green pepper, deseeded and sliced

225 g/8 oz pineapple pieces

1 small carrot, cut into thin strips

25 g/1 oz canned bamboo shoots, drained, rinsed and halved

freshly cooked rice, to serve

BATTER

125 g/4½ oz plain flour

1 tbsp cornflour

1½ tsp baking powder

1 tbsp vegetable oil

SAUCE

125 g/4½ oz soft light brown sugar

2 tbsp cornflour

125 ml/4 fl oz white wine vinegar

2 garlic cloves, crushed

4 tbsp tomato purée

6 tbsp pineapple juice

1. To make the batter, sift the plain flour into a mixing bowl, together with the cornflour and baking powder. Add the oil and stir in enough water to make a thick, smooth batter (about 175 ml/6 fl oz).

2. Pour the vegetable oil into a preheated wok and heat until almost smoking.

3. Dip the cubes of pork into the batter and cook in the hot oil, in batches, until the pork is cooked through. Remove the pork from the wok with a slotted spoon and drain on kitchen paper. Set aside and keep warm until required.

4. Drain all but 1 tablespoon of oil from the wok and return it to the heat. Add the onion, pepper, pineapple pieces, carrot and bamboo shoots and stir-fry for 1–2 minutes. Remove from the wok with a slotted spoon and set aside. Mix all of the sauce ingredients together and pour into the wok.

5. Bring to the boil, stirring until thickened and clear. Cook for 1 minute, then return the pork and vegetables to the wok. Cook for a further 1–2 minutes, then transfer to a serving plate and serve with freshly cooked rice.

Soft-wrapped Pork and Prawn Rolls

MAKES 20

115 g/4 oz firm tofu

3 tbsp vegetable or groundnut oil

1 tsp finely chopped garlic

55 g/2 oz lean pork, shredded

115 g/4 oz raw prawns, peeled and deveined

½ small carrot, cut into short, thin sticks

55 g/2 oz canned bamboo shoots, rinsed and shredded

115 g/4 oz very finely sliced cabbage

55 g/2 oz mangetout, julienned

1-egg omelette, shredded

1 tsp salt

1 tsp light soy sauce

1 tsp Chinese rice wine

pinch of white pepper

20 soft spring roll wrappers

chilli bean sauce, to serve

1. Slice the tofu horizontally into thin slices. Heat 1 tablespoon of the oil in a large frying pan and cook the tofu for 4–5 minutes, turning occasionally, until golden brown all over. Cut into thin strips and set aside.

2. In a preheated wok or deep saucepan, heat the remaining oil and stir-fry the garlic until fragrant. Add the pork and stir for about 1 minute, then add the prawns and stir for a further minute. One by one, stirring well after each addition, add the carrot, bamboo shoots, cabbage, mangetout, tofu and, finally, the shredded omelette. Season with the salt, soy sauce, rice wine and pepper. Stir for one more minute, then turn into a serving dish.

3. To assemble each roll, smear a wrapper with a little chilli bean sauce and place a heaped teaspoon of the filling towards the bottom of the circle. Roll up the bottom edge to secure the filling, turn in the sides and continue to roll up gently. Serve accompanied by a bowl of chilli bean sauce.

Pork and Ginger Dumplings

MAKES 50

450 g/1 lb pork mince, not too lean

1 tbsp light soy sauce

1½ tsp salt

1 tsp Chinese rice wine

½ tsp sesame oil

100 g/3½ oz very finely chopped cabbage

2 tsp minced fresh ginger

2 tsp finely chopped spring onions

½ tsp white pepper

50 round wonton wrappers,
    about 7 cm/2¾ inches in diameter

flour, for dusting

DIPPING SAUCE

1 tbsp soy sauce

1 tbsp rice vinegar

½ tsp sugar

1 tsp chopped fresh ginger

1 tsp chopped garlic

1. To make the dipping sauce, stir all the ingredients together and set aside.

2. For the filling, mix the pork with the light soy sauce and ½ teaspoon of the salt. Stir carefully, always in the same direction, to create a thick paste. Add the rice wine and sesame oil and continue mixing in the same direction. Cover and leave to rest for at least 20 minutes.

3. Meanwhile, sprinkle the cabbage with the remaining salt to help draw out the water. Add the ginger, spring onions and white pepper and knead for at least 5 minutes into a thick paste. Combine with the filling.

4. To make the dumplings, place about 1 tablespoon of the filling in the centre of each wrapper, holding the wrapper in the palm of one hand. Moisten the edges with water, then seal the edges with 2–3 pleats on each side and place on a lightly floured board.

5. To cook the dumplings, bring 1 litre/1¾ pints of water to a rolling boil in a large saucepan. Drop in about 20 dumplings at a time, stirring gently with a chopstick to prevent them sticking together. Cover, then bring back to the boil and cook for 2 minutes. Uncover and add about 200 ml/7 fl oz of cold water. Bring back to the boil, cover and cook for a further 2 minutes. Serve the dumplings with individual bowls of dipping sauce.

Sweet and Sour Spare Ribs

SERVES 4

450 g/1 lb spare ribs, cut into bite-sized pieces

1½ tbsp vegetable or groundnut oil, plus extra
  for deep-frying

1 green pepper, deseeded and
  roughly chopped

1 small onion, roughly chopped

1 small carrot, finely sliced

½ tsp finely chopped garlic

½ tsp finely chopped fresh ginger

100 g/3½ oz pineapple chunks

MARINADE

2 tsp light soy sauce

½ tsp salt

pinch of white pepper

SAUCE

3 tbsp white rice vinegar

2 tbsp sugar

1 tbsp light soy sauce

1 tbsp tomato ketchup

1. Combine all the marinade ingredients in a bowl. Add the pork and leave to marinate for at least 20 minutes.

2. Heat enough oil for deep-frying in a wok, deep-fat fryer or large heavy-based saucepan to 180–190°C/350–375°F, or until a cube of bread browns in 30 seconds. Deep-fry the spare ribs for 8 minutes. Drain and set aside.

3. To prepare the sauce, mix together the vinegar, sugar, light soy sauce and ketchup. Set aside.

4. In a preheated wok, heat 1 tablespoon of the oil and stir-fry the pepper, onion and carrot for 2 minutes. Remove and set aside. Wipe the wok clean.

5. In the clean preheated wok, heat ½ tablespoon oil and stir-fry the garlic and root ginger until fragrant. Add the sauce. Bring back to the boil and add the pineapple chunks. Finally add the spare ribs and the pepper, onion and carrot. Stir until warmed through and serve immediately.

Pork and Crab Meatballs

SERVES 6

225 g/8 oz pork fillet, finely chopped
170 g/5¾ oz canned crabmeat, drained
3 spring onions, finely chopped
1 garlic clove, finely chopped
1 tsp Thai red curry paste
1 tbsp cornflour
1 egg white
vegetable or groundnut oil, for deep-frying
freshly cooked rice, to serve

SAUCE
1 tbsp vegetable or groundnut oil
2 shallots, chopped
1 garlic clove, crushed
2 large fresh red chillies, deseeded and
   chopped
4 spring onions, chopped
3 tomatoes, roughly chopped

1. Put the pork and crabmeat into a bowl and mix together. Add the spring onions, garlic, curry paste, cornflour and egg white and beat together well to make a thick paste. With damp hands, shape the mixture into walnut-sized balls.

2. Heat enough oil for deep-frying in a wok, deep-fat fryer or large heavy-based saucepan to 180–190°C/350–375°F, or until a cube of bread browns in 30 seconds. Deep-fry the balls, in batches, for 3–4 minutes, turning frequently, until golden brown and cooked. Drain on kitchen paper and keep warm.

3. To make the sauce, heat the oil in a wok and stir-fry the shallots and garlic for 1–2 minutes. Add the chillies and spring onions and stir-fry for 1–2 minutes, then add the tomatoes. Stir together quickly, then spoon the sauce over the pork-and-crab balls. Serve immediately with freshly cooked rice.

Stir-fried Lamb with Orange

SERVES 4

450 g/1 lb minced lamb

2 garlic cloves, crushed

1 tsp cumin seeds

1 tsp ground coriander

1 red onion, sliced

finely grated rind and juice of 1 orange

2 tbsp soy sauce

1 orange, peeled and segmented

salt and pepper

snipped fresh chives, to garnish

1. Heat a wok or large frying pan, without adding any oil. Add the minced lamb to the wok. Dry-fry the minced lamb for 5 minutes, or until evenly browned. Drain away any excess fat from the wok.

2. Add the garlic, cumin seeds, coriander and red onion to the wok and stir-fry for a further 5 minutes.

3. Stir in the finely grated orange rind and juice and the soy sauce, mixing until thoroughly combined. Cover, reduce the heat and leave to simmer, stirring occasionally, for 15 minutes.

4. Remove the lid, increase the heat and add the orange segments. Stir to mix.

5. Season with salt and pepper to taste and heat through for a further 2–3 minutes. Transfer the stir-fry to warm serving plates and garnish with snipped fresh chives. Serve immediately.

Lamb with Black Bean Sauce

SERVES 4

450 g/1 lb lamb neck fillet or boneless
  leg of lamb chops

1 egg white, lightly beaten

4 tbsp cornflour

1 tsp Chinese five-spice powder

3 tbsp sunflower oil

1 red onion, sliced

1 red pepper, deseeded and sliced

1 green pepper, deseeded and sliced

1 yellow or orange pepper, deseeded and
  sliced

5 tbsp black bean sauce

freshly cooked noodles, to serve

1. Using a sharp knife, slice the lamb into very thin strips.

2. Mix together the egg white, cornflour and Chinese five-spice powder. Toss the lamb strips in the mixture until evenly coated.

3. Heat the oil in a preheated wok or large frying pan and stir-fry the lamb over a high heat for 5 minutes, or until it crispens around the edges.

4. Add the onion and pepper slices to the wok and stir-fry for 5–6 minutes, or until the vegetables just begin to soften.

5. Stir the black bean sauce into the mixture in the wok and heat through.

6. Transfer the lamb and sauce to warm serving plates and serve hot with freshly cooked noodles.

Beef Chop Suey

SERVES 4

450 g/1 lb ribeye or sirloin steak, finely sliced

1 head of broccoli, cut into small florets

2 tbsp vegetable or groundnut oil

1 onion, finely sliced

2 celery sticks, finely sliced diagonally

225 g/8 oz mangetout, sliced in half lengthways

55 g/2 oz canned bamboo shoots,
   rinsed and julienned

8 canned water chestnuts, drained and
   finely sliced

225 g/8 oz finely sliced mushrooms

1 tbsp oyster sauce

1 tsp salt

MARINADE

1 tbsp Chinese rice wine

pinch of white pepper

pinch of salt

1 tbsp light soy sauce

½ tsp sesame oil

1. Combine all the marinade ingredients in a bowl and marinate the beef for at least 20 minutes. Blanch the broccoli florets in a large saucepan of boiling water for 30 seconds. Drain and set aside.

2. In a preheated wok or deep saucepan, heat 1 tablespoon of the oil and stir-fry the beef until the colour has changed. Remove and set aside.

3. In the clean wok or deep saucepan, heat the remaining oil and stir-fry the onion for 1 minute. Add the celery and broccoli and cook for 2 minutes. Add the mangetout, bamboo shoots, chestnuts and mushrooms and cook for 1 minute. Add the beef, then season with the oyster sauce and salt and serve immediately.

Beef Chow Mein

SERVES 4

280 g/10 oz fillet steak, cut into slivers

225 g/8 oz dried egg noodles

2 tbsp vegetable or groundnut oil

1 onion, finely sliced

1 green pepper, deseeded and finely sliced

140 g/5 oz fresh beansprouts, trimmed

1 tsp salt

pinch of sugar

2 tsp Chinese rice wine

2 tbsp light soy sauce

1 tbsp dark soy sauce

1 tbsp finely shredded spring onion

MARINADE

1 tsp light soy sauce

dash of sesame oil

½ tsp Chinese rice wine

pinch of white pepper

1. Combine all the marinade ingredients in a bowl and marinate the beef for at least 20 minutes.

2. Cook the noodles according to the instructions on the packet. When cooked, rinse under cold water and set aside.

3. In a preheated wok or deep pan, heat the oil and stir-fry the beef for about 1 minute, until the meat has changed colour, then add the onion and cook for 1 minute, followed by the pepper and beansprouts. Evaporate off any water from the vegetables. Add the salt, sugar, rice wine and soy sauces. Stir in the noodles and toss for 1 minute. Finally, stir in the spring onion and serve.

Sweet and Sour Chicken

SERVES 4–6

450 g/1 lb lean chicken, cubed
5 tbsp vegetable or groundnut oil
½ tsp crushed garlic
½ tsp finely chopped fresh ginger
1 green pepper, deseeded and
  roughly chopped
1 onion, roughly chopped
1 carrot, finely sliced
1 tsp sesame oil
1 tbsp finely chopped spring onion
freshly cooked rice, to serve

MARINADE
2 tsp light soy sauce
1 tsp Chinese rice wine
pinch of white pepper
½ tsp salt
dash of sesame oil

SAUCE
8 tbsp rice vinegar
4 tbsp sugar
2 tsp light soy sauce
6 tbsp tomato ketchup

1. Combine all the marinade ingredients in a bowl and marinate the chicken pieces for at least 20 minutes.

2. To prepare the sauce, heat the vinegar in a pan and add the sugar, light soy sauce and tomato ketchup. Stir to dissolve the sugar, then set aside.

3. In a preheated wok or large frying pan, heat 3 tablespoons of the oil and stir-fry the chicken until it starts to turn golden brown. Remove and set aside. Wipe the wok clean.

4. In the clean wok, heat the remaining oil and cook the garlic and ginger until fragrant. Add the vegetables and cook for 2 minutes. Add the chicken and cook for 1 minute. Finally add the sauce and the sesame oil, then stir in the spring onion and serve immediately with freshly cooked rice.

Gong Bau Chicken

SERVES 4

2 boneless chicken breasts, with or without
    skin, cut into 1-cm/½-inch cubes

1 tbsp vegetable or groundnut oil

10 dried red chillies or more, to taste, snipped
    into 2–3 pieces

1 tsp Szechuan peppers

3 garlic cloves, finely sliced

2.5-cm/1-inch piece fresh ginger,
    finely sliced

1 tbsp roughly chopped spring onion,
    white part only

85 g/3 oz peanuts, roasted

MARINADE

2 tsp light soy sauce

1 tsp Chinese rice wine

½ tsp sugar

SAUCE

1 tsp light soy sauce

1 tsp dark soy sauce

1 tsp black rice vinegar

a few drops of sesame oil

2 tbsp chicken stock

1 tsp sugar

1. Combine all the marinade ingredients in a bowl and marinate the chicken, covered, for at least
    20 minutes. Combine all the ingredients for the sauce and set aside.

2. In a preheated wok or large frying pan, heat the oil and stir-fry the chillies and peppers until crisp
    and fragrant. Toss in the chicken pieces. When they begin to turn white, add the garlic, ginger and
    spring onion. Stir-fry for about 5 minutes, or until the chicken is cooked.

3. Pour in the sauce, mix together thoroughly, then stir in the peanuts. Serve immediately.

Chicken and Shiitake Mushrooms

SERVES 4

2 tbsp vegetable oil

1 lb 8 oz chicken breast, skinned and cut into
  2.5-cm/1-inch chunks

1 tsp grated fresh ginger

3 carrots, thinly sliced

2 onions, thinly sliced

100 g/3½ oz fresh beansprouts

225 g/8 oz fresh or dried shiitake mushrooms,
  thinly sliced

3 tbsp chopped fresh coriander

freshly cooked noodles, to serve

SAUCE

175 g/6 oz white sugar

225 ml/8 fl oz soy sauce

1 tsp Chinese five-spice powder

225 ml/8 fl oz sweet sherry

1. To make the sauce, combine the sugar, soy sauce, Chinese five-spice powder and sherry in a bowl.
   Mix well and set aside.

2. In a preheated wok or large frying pan, heat the oil over a medium–high heat. Add the chicken and
   stir-fry for 2 minutes, then add the ginger and fry for 1 minute, stirring continuously. Add the sauce
   and cook for a further 2 minutes.

3. One ingredient at a time, add the carrots, onions, beansprouts, mushrooms and coriander. Stir-fry
   after each addition.

4. Once the sauce has reduced and is thick, transfer the stir-fry to warmed serving bowls. Serve
   immediately with noodles.

Cross the Bridge Noodles

SERVES 4

300 g/10½ oz dried fine egg noodles
  or rice sticks
200 g/7 oz choi sum or similar green vegetable
2 litres/3½ pints chicken stock
1-cm/½-inch piece fresh ginger, peeled
1–2 tsp salt

1 tsp sugar
1 boneless, skinless chicken breast, finely sliced
  diagonally
200 g/7 oz white fish fillet, finely sliced
  diagonally
1 tbsp light soy sauce

1. Cook the noodles according to the instructions on the packet. When cooked, rinse under cold water and set aside. Blanch the choi sum in a large saucepan of boiling water for 30 seconds. Rinse under cold water and set aside.

2. In a large saucepan, bring the stock to the boil, then add the ginger, 1 teaspoon of the salt and the sugar and skim the surface. Add the chicken and cook for about 4 minutes, then add the fish and simmer for a further 4 minutes, or until the fish and chicken are cooked through.

3. Add the noodles and choi sum with the light soy sauce and bring back to the boil. Taste and adjust the seasoning if necessary. Serve immediately in large individual noodle bowls.

Chicken with Cashew Nuts

SERVES 4–6

450 g/1 lb boneless chicken meat,
  cut into bite-sized pieces
2 dried Chinese mushrooms, soaked in warm
  water for 20 minutes
2 tbsp vegetable or groundnut oil
4 slices fresh ginger
1 tsp finely chopped garlic
1 red pepper, deseeded and cut into 2.5-cm/
  1-inch squares

1 tbsp light soy sauce
85 g/3 oz cashew nuts, roasted

MARINADE
1 tsp Chinese rice wine
pinch of sugar
½ tsp salt
2 tbsp light soy sauce

1. Combine all the marinade ingredients in a bowl and marinate the chicken for at least 20 minutes.

2. Squeeze any excess water from the mushrooms and slice finely, discarding any tough stems.
    Reserve the soaking water.

3. In a preheated wok, heat 1 tablespoon of the oil. Add the ginger and stir-fry until fragrant. Stir in
    the chicken and cook for 2 minutes, or until it begins to turn brown. Before the chicken is cooked
    through, remove and set aside. Wipe the wok clean.

4. In the clean wok, heat the remaining oil and stir-fry the garlic until fragrant. Add the mushrooms
    and red pepper and stir-fry for 1 minute. Add about 2 tablespoons of the mushroom-soaking water
    and cook for about 2 minutes, or until the water has evaporated.

5. Return the chicken to the wok, then add the remaining light soy sauce and the cashew nuts and
    stir-fry for 2 minutes, or until the chicken is cooked through.

Chicken Fried Rice

SERVES 4

½ tbsp sesame oil

6 shallots, peeled and cut into quarters

450 g/1 lb cooked chicken, cubed

3 tbsp soy sauce

2 carrots, diced

1 celery stick, diced

1 red pepper, deseeded and diced

175 g/6 oz fresh peas

100 g/3½ oz canned sweetcorn, drained

275 g/9¾ oz cooked long-grain rice

2 large eggs, scrambled

1. Heat the oil in a preheated wok or large frying pan over a medium heat. Add the shallots and fry until soft, then add the chicken and 2 tablespoons of the soy sauce and stir-fry for 5–6 minutes.

2. Stir in the carrots, celery, red pepper, peas and sweetcorn and stir-fry for a further 5 minutes. Add the rice and stir thoroughly.

3. Finally, stir in the scrambled eggs and the remaining tablespoon of soy sauce. Serve immediately.

Peking Duck

SERVES 6–10

1 duck, weighing 2 kg/4 lb 8 oz

1.7 litres/3 pints boiling water

1 tbsp honey

1 tbsp Chinese rice wine

1 tsp white rice vinegar

TO SERVE

1 cucumber, peeled, deseeded and julienned

10 spring onions, white part only, shredded

30 Peking duck pancakes

plum or hoisin sauce, or both

1. To prepare the duck, massage the skin to loosen it from the meat.

2. Pour the boiling water into a large saucepan, then add the honey, rice wine and vinegar and lower in the duck. Baste for about 1 minute. Remove the duck and hang it to dry for a few hours or overnight.

3. Preheat the oven to 200°C/400°F/Gas Mark 5. Place the duck on a rack above a roasting tin and roast for at least 1 hour, or until the skin is very crispy and the duck cooked through.

4. To serve, bring the duck to the table, together with the cucumber, spring onions and pancakes, and carve off the skin first. On a pancake, arrange a little skin with some cucumber and spring onion pieces. Top with a little plum or hoisin sauce, or both. Roll up and eat. Repeat the process with the lean meat.

Fruity Duck Stir-fry

SERVES 4

4 duck breasts
1 tsp Chinese five-spice powder
1 tbsp cornflour
1 tbsp chilli oil
225 g/8 oz baby onions, peeled
2 garlic cloves, crushed

100 g/3½ oz baby corn
175 g/6 oz canned pineapple chunks
6 spring onions, sliced
100 g/3½ oz fresh beansprouts
2 tbsp plum sauce

1. Remove any skin from the duck breasts. Cut the duck into thin slices.

2. Mix the Chinese five-spice powder and the cornflour. Toss the duck in the mixture until well coated.

3. Heat the oil in a preheated wok. Stir-fry the duck for 10 minutes, or until just beginning to crispen around the edges. Remove from the wok and set aside.

4. Add the onions and garlic to the wok and stir-fry for 5 minutes, or until softened. Add the baby corn and stir-fry for a further 5 minutes. Add the pineapple, spring onions and beansprouts and stir-fry for 3–4 minutes. Stir in the plum sauce.

5. Return the cooked duck to the wok and toss until well mixed. Transfer to warm serving dishes and serve hot.

Turkey, Broccoli and Pak Choi

SERVES 4

450 g/1 lb turkey breast, cut into strips

1 tbsp vegetable oil

1 head of broccoli, cut into florets

2 heads of pak choi, leaves washed and separated (or savoy cabbage, if pak choi is unavailable)

1 red pepper, deseeded and thinly sliced

50 ml/2 fl oz chicken stock

MARINADE

1 tbsp soy sauce

1 tbsp honey

2 garlic cloves, crushed

1. Combine all the marinade ingredients in a bowl, add the turkey and toss to coat. Cover the bowl with clingfilm and marinate in the refrigerator for 2 hours.

2. Put a wok or large frying pan over a medium–high heat, add the oil and heat for 1 minute. Add the turkey and stir-fry for 3 minutes, or until the turkey is opaque. Remove with a slotted spoon, set aside and keep warm.

3. Add the broccoli, pak choi and red pepper to the pan and stir-fry for 2 minutes. Add the stock and continue to stir-fry for 2 minutes, or until the vegetables are crisp but tender.

4. Return the turkey to the wok and cook briefly to reheat. Serve immediately.

Turkey with Bamboo Shoots and Water Chestnuts

SERVES 4

450 g/1 lb turkey breast, cubed
1 tbsp sesame oil
125 g/4½ oz small mushrooms, halved
1 green pepper, deseeded and cut into strips
1 courgette, thinly sliced
4 spring onions, cut into quarters
115 g/4 oz canned bamboo shoots, drained
115 g/4 oz canned water chestnuts,
    drained and sliced

MARINADE
4 tbsp sweet sherry
1 tbsp lemon juice
1 tbsp soy sauce
2 tsp grated fresh ginger
1 garlic clove, crushed

1. Combine all the marinade ingredients in a bowl, then add the turkey and stir. Cover with clingfilm and marinate in the refrigerator for 3–4 hours.

2. Heat the oil in a preheated wok or large frying pan. Remove the turkey from the marinade with a slotted spoon (reserving the marinade) and stir-fry a few pieces at a time until browned. Remove the turkey from the wok and set aside.

3. Add the mushrooms, pepper and courgette to the wok and stir-fry for 3 minutes. Add the spring onions and stir-fry for a further minute. Add the bamboo shoots and water chestnuts to the wok, then add the turkey and half the reserved marinade. Stir over a medium–high heat for a further 2–3 minutes, until the ingredients are evenly coated and the marinade has reduced.

4. Serve immediately in warmed bowls.

Fish and Seafood Dishes

China's extensive coastline and inland waterways offer a huge variety of fresh- and salt-water fish and seafood. Favourites include pike, carp, mandarin fish (a type of perch), shad and grouper, plus many other varieties familiar in the West. Prawns are widely consumed, and scallops, squid and clams cooked in spicy sauces are also popular.

Somewhat surprisingly, fresh-water fish and shellfish play a much bigger part in the Chinese diet than those from the sea, despite 3,800 miles/4,800 km of coastline. This is partly because much of it is farmed in special ponds that are restocked each year, but also because fresh-water fish, especially crabs and prawns, are considered sweeter and more delicate than salt-water equivalents. Soft-shell fresh-water crabs, in particular, are highly prized in Beijing.

The Chinese like to cook their fish whole, either steamed, quickly poached in boiling broth or water, or deep-fried. Lobster and crab are sometimes fried in flavoured oil that penetrates the cracked shells, creating the most delectable sauce that the Chinese love to suck from the shells.

Though fish and seafood are commonplace in the kitchen, the Chinese do not like fishy smells. Ginger, garlic and salty black bean sauce are often used to disguise such smells. Freshness is paramount – no respectable cook would dream of buying anything but a live fish, purchased in a leak-proof basket and kept alive until just before cooking. While this is not usually possible in the West, it is advisable to purchase fish and seafood from a reputable fishmonger. Fresh fish should never smell fishy – this is a sign that it's past its best.

Seafood Chow Mein

SERVES 4

85 g/3 oz squid, cleaned

3–4 fresh scallops

85 g/3 oz raw prawns, peeled

½ egg white, lightly beaten

2 tsp cornflour, mixed to a paste with
   2½ tsp water

275 g/9¾ oz dried fine egg noodles

5–6 tbsp vegetable oil

2 tbsp light soy sauce

55 g/2 oz mangetout, sliced diagonally

½ tsp salt

½ tsp sugar

1 tsp Chinese rice wine

2 spring onions, finely shredded

a few drops of sesame oil

1. Open up the squid and score the inside in a criss-cross pattern, then cut into pieces about 2.5 cm/ 1 inch square. Soak the squid in a bowl of boiling water until all the pieces curl up. Rinse in cold water and drain.

2. Cut each scallop into 3–4 slices. Cut the prawns in half lengthways if large. Mix the scallops and prawns with the egg white and cornflour paste.

3. Cook the noodles according to the instructions on the packet, then drain and rinse under cold water. Drain well, then toss with about 1 tablespoon of the oil.

4. Heat 3 tablespoons of the oil in a preheated wok. Add the noodles and 1 tablespoon of the soy sauce and stir-fry for 2–3 minutes. Remove to a large serving dish.

5. Heat the remaining oil in the wok and add the mangetout and seafood. Stir-fry for about 2 minutes, then add the salt, sugar, rice wine, the remaining soy sauce and about half the spring onions. Blend well and add a little water if necessary. Pour the seafood mixture on top of the noodles and sprinkle with sesame oil. Garnish with the remaining spring onions and serve immediately.

Five-willow Fish

SERVES 4–6

1 whole sea bass or similar, weighing
  450–675 g/1 lb–1 lb 8 oz, gutted
2 tsp salt
6 tbsp vegetable or groundnut oil
2 slices fresh ginger
2 garlic cloves, finely sliced
2 spring onions, roughly chopped
1 green pepper, deseeded and thinly sliced
1 red pepper, deseeded and thinly sliced

1 carrot, finely sliced
55 g/2 oz canned bamboo shoots,
  rinsed and thinly sliced
2 tomatoes, peeled, deseeded and thinly sliced
1 tbsp Chinese rice wine
2 tbsp white rice vinegar
1 tbsp light soy sauce
1 tbsp sugar

1. Clean the fish and dry thoroughly. Score the fish on both sides with deep, diagonal cuts. Press ½ teaspoon of the salt into the skin.

2. In a preheated wok, heat 4 tablespoons of the oil and cook the fish for about 4 minutes on each side or until the flesh is soft. Drain, then set aside on a warmed dish and keep warm. Wipe the wok clean.

3. Preheat the clean wok, then heat the remaining oil and stir-fry the ginger, garlic and spring onions until fragrant. Toss in the vegetables with the remaining salt and stir rapidly for 2–3 minutes. Add the remaining ingredients and mix well for 2–3 minutes. Pour the sauce over the fish and serve immediately.

Salmon and Scallops with Coriander and Lime

SERVES 4

6 tbsp groundnut oil

280 g/10 oz salmon steak, skinned and cut into
   2.5-cm/1-inch chunks

225 g/8 oz scallops

3 carrots, thinly sliced

2 celery stalks, cut into 2.5-cm/1-inch pieces

2 yellow peppers, deseeded and thinly sliced

175 g/6 oz oyster mushrooms, thinly sliced

1 garlic clove, crushed

6 tbsp chopped fresh coriander

3 shallots, thinly sliced

juice of 2 limes

1 tsp lime zest

1 tsp dried red pepper flakes

3 tbsp dry sherry

3 tbsp soy sauce

1. In a preheated wok or large frying pan, heat the oil over a medium heat. Add the salmon and scallops and stir-fry for 3 minutes. Remove from the wok, set aside and keep warm.

2. Add the carrots, celery, peppers, mushrooms and garlic to the wok and stir-fry for 3 minutes. Add the coriander and shallots and stir.

3. Add the lime juice and zest, dried red pepper flakes, sherry and soy sauce and stir. Return the salmon and scallops to the wok and stir-fry carefully for another minute. Serve immediately.

Ginger-marinated Salmon and Scallop Skewers

SERVES 4

RICE SALAD
200 g/7 oz brown basmati rice

½ cucumber, diced

4 spring onions, sliced

½ bunch fresh coriander, chopped

1 red pepper, deseeded and diced

1 fresh green chilli, deseeded and thinly sliced

juice of 1 lime

2 tbsp sesame oil

SKEWERS
500 g/1 lb 2 oz salmon fillet, skinned and
   cut into chunks

8 prepared scallops

4-cm/1½-inch piece fresh ginger

juice of 1 lemon

1 tbsp olive oil

salad leaves, to serve

1. Bring a large pan of water to the boil, add the rice, and cook for 25 minutes, or until tender. Drain and leave to cool. Mix the cooled rice with the cucumber, spring onions, coriander, red pepper, chilli, lime juice and sesame oil in a bowl. Cover and set aside for the flavours to develop.

2. Meanwhile, put the salmon chunks and scallops into a shallow, non-metallic bowl. Using a garlic press or the back of a knife, crush the ginger to extract the juice. Mix the ginger juice with the lemon juice and olive oil in a small bowl or jug and pour over the seafood. Turn the seafood to coat in the marinade. Cover and leave to marinate in the refrigerator for 30 minutes. Soak 8 wooden skewers in cold water for 30 minutes, then drain.

3. Preheat the grill to high. Thread the salmon and scallops onto the skewers. Cook under the preheated grill for 3–4 minutes on each side, or until cooked through.

4. Serve the hot seafood skewers with the rice salad and salad leaves.

Monkfish Stir-fry

SERVES 4

2 tsp sesame oil

450 g/1 lb monkfish steaks, cut into
   2.5-cm/1-inch chunks

1 onion, thinly sliced

3 garlic cloves, finely chopped

1 tsp grated fresh ginger

225 g/8 oz fine tip asparagus

175 g/6 oz mushrooms, thinly sliced

2 tbsp soy sauce

1 tbsp lemon juice

1. Heat the oil in a preheated wok or large frying pan over a medium–high heat. Add the fish, onion, garlic, ginger, asparagus and mushrooms. Stir-fry for 2–3 minutes.

2. Stir in the soy sauce and lemon juice and cook for a further minute. Remove from the heat and transfer to warm serving dishes. Serve immediately.

Fried Fish with Pine Kernels

SERVES 4–6

½ tsp salt

450 g/1 lb thick white fish fillets, cut into
2.5-cm/1-inch cubes

2 dried Chinese mushrooms, soaked in warm
water for 20 minutes

3 tbsp vegetable or groundnut oil

2.5-cm/1-inch piece fresh ginger,
finely shredded

1 tbsp chopped spring onion

1 red pepper, deseeded and cut into 2.5-cm/
1-inch squares

1 green pepper, deseeded and cut into
2.5-cm/1-inch squares

25 g/1 oz canned bamboo shoots, rinsed and
cut into small cubes

2 tsp Chinese rice wine

2 tbsp pine kernels, toasted

freshly cooked rice, to serve

1. Sprinkle the salt over the fish and set aside for 20 minutes. Squeeze out any excess water from the mushrooms and slice finely, discarding any tough stems.

2. In a preheated wok or large frying pan, heat 2 tablespoons of the oil and stir-fry the fish for 3 minutes. Drain the fish and set aside, then wipe the wok clean.

3. Preheat the clean wok and heat the remaining oil, then toss in the ginger. Stir until fragrant, then add the spring onion, peppers, bamboo shoots, mushrooms and rice wine and cook for 1–2 minutes.

4. Finally add the fish and stir to warm through. Sprinkle with pine kernels and serve with freshly cooked rice.

Sweet and Sour Sea Bass

SERVES 2

60 g/2¼ oz pak choi, shredded

40 g/1½ oz fresh beansprouts

40 g/1½ oz shiitake mushrooms, sliced

40 g/1½ oz oyster mushrooms, torn

20 g/¾ oz spring onions, finely sliced

1 tsp finely grated fresh ginger

1 tbsp finely sliced lemon grass

2 x 90 g/3¼ oz sea bass fillets, skinned and boned

10 g/¼ oz sesame seeds, toasted

SWEET AND SOUR SAUCE

90 ml/3 fl oz pineapple juice

1 tbsp sugar

1 tbsp red wine vinegar

2 star anise, crushed

90 ml/3 fl oz tomato juice

1 tbsp cornflour, blended with a little cold water

1. Preheat the oven to 200°C/400°F/Gas Mark 6. Cut out 2 x 38-cm/15-inch squares of greaseproof paper and 2 x 38-cm/15-inch squares of foil.

2. To make the sauce, heat the pineapple juice, sugar, vinegar, star anise and tomato juice in a saucepan and simmer for 1–2 minutes. Thicken with the cornflour and water mixture, whisking constantly, then pass through a fine sieve into a small bowl to cool.

3. In a separate large bowl mix together the pak choi, beansprouts, mushrooms and spring onions, then add the ginger and lemon grass. Toss all the ingredients together.

4. Put a square of greaseproof paper on top of a square of foil and fold into a triangle. Open up and place half the vegetable mix in the centre, pour half the sweet and sour sauce over the vegetables and place the sea bass on top. Sprinkle with a few sesame seeds. Close the triangle over the mixture and crumple the edges together to form an airtight triangular parcel. Repeat to make the second parcel.

5. Place the foil parcels on a baking tray and cook in the preheated oven for 10 minutes, until they puff with steam. Transfer the contents of each parcel to an individual plate and serve immediately.

Deep-fried River Fish with Chilli Bean Sauce

SERVES 4–6

1 whole freshwater fish, such as trout or carp,
 weighing 400 g/14 oz, gutted
1 heaped tbsp plain flour
pinch of salt
100 ml/3½ fl oz water
vegetable or groundnut oil, for deep-frying

SAUCE
100 ml/3½ fl oz vegetable or groundnut oil
1 tsp dried chilli flakes
1 garlic clove, finely chopped
1 tsp finely chopped fresh ginger
1 tbsp chilli bean sauce
½ tsp white pepper
2 tsp sugar
1 tbsp white rice vinegar
1 tsp finely chopped spring onion

1. To prepare the fish, clean and dry thoroughly. Mix together the flour, salt and water to create a light batter. Coat the fish.

2. Heat enough oil for deep-frying in a wok, deep-fat fryer or large heavy-based saucepan to 180–190°C/350–375°F, or until a cube of bread browns in 30 seconds. Deep-fry the fish until the skin is crisp and golden brown. Drain, set aside and keep warm.

3. To make the sauce, first heat all but 1 tablespoon of the oil in a small pan and, when smoking, pour over the dried chilli flakes. Set aside.

4. In a preheated wok or deep pan, heat the remaining oil and stir-fry the garlic and ginger until fragrant. Stir in the chilli bean sauce, then add the oil-chilli flake mixture. Season with the pepper, sugar and vinegar. Turn off the heat and stir in the spring onion. Tip over the fish and serve immediately.

Wok-fried King Prawns in Spicy Sauce

SERVES 4

3 tbsp vegetable or groundnut oil

450 g/1 lb raw king prawns, deveined but unpeeled

2 tsp finely chopped fresh ginger

1 tsp finely chopped garlic

1 tbsp chopped spring onion

2 tbsp chilli bean sauce

1 tsp Chinese rice wine

1 tsp sugar

½ tsp light soy sauce

1–2 tbsp chicken stock

1. In a preheated wok, heat the oil, then add the prawns and stir-fry over high heat for about 4 minutes. Arrange the prawns on the sides of the wok out of the oil, then add the ginger and garlic and stir until fragrant. Add the spring onion and chilli bean sauce. Stir the prawns into this mixture.

2. Lower the heat slightly and add the rice wine, sugar, soy sauce and stock. Cover and cook for a further minute. Serve immediately.

Ginger Prawns with Oyster Mushrooms

SERVES 4

3–4 tbsp vegetable oil
3 carrots, thinly sliced
350 g/12 oz oyster mushrooms, thinly sliced
1 large red pepper, deseeded and thinly sliced
450g/1 lb large prawns, peeled
2 garlic cloves, crushed
fresh coriander leaves, to garnish
freshly cooked rice, to serve

SAUCE
150 ml/5 fl oz chicken stock
2 tsp sesame seeds
3 tsp grated fresh ginger
1 tbsp light soy sauce
¼ tsp hot pepper sauce
1 tsp cornflour

1. To make the sauce, stir together the stock, sesame seeds, ginger, soy sauce, hot pepper sauce and cornflour in a small bowl until well blended. Set aside.

2. In a preheated wok or large frying pan, heat 2 tablespoons of the oil. Stir-fry the carrots for 3 minutes, remove from the pan and set aside.

3. Add 1 tablespoon of the remaining oil to the wok and stir-fry the mushrooms for 2 minutes. Remove from the pan and set aside.

4. Add the remaining oil if needed and stir-fry the pepper with the prawns and garlic for 3 minutes, until the prawns turn pink and opaque.

5. Stir the sauce and pour it into the wok. Cook until the mixture bubbles, then return the carrots and mushrooms to the wok. Cover and cook for a further 2 minutes, until heated through.

6. Garnish with coriander leaves and serve immediately with freshly cooked rice.

Prawns Fu Yung

SERVES 4–6

1 tbsp vegetable or groundnut oil
115 g/4 oz large prawns, peeled and deveined
4 eggs, lightly beaten

1 tsp salt
pinch of white pepper
2 tbsp finely chopped Chinese chives

1. In a preheated wok, heat the oil and stir-fry the prawns until they begin to turn pink.

2. Season the eggs with the salt and pepper and pour over the prawns. Stir-fry for 1 minute, then add the chives.

3. Cook for a further 4 minutes, stirring all the time, until the eggs are cooked through but still soft in texture. Serve immediately.

Drunken Prawns

SERVES 4–6

200 g/7 oz jumbo prawns, peeled and deveined
100 ml/3½ fl oz Chinese rice wine
2 tbsp brandy

½ tsp salt
1 tbsp finely chopped spring onion
1 tsp finely chopped fresh ginger

1. Blanch the prawns in a large pan of boiling water for 30 seconds. Drain and set aside.

2. Combine all the ingredients, cover and leave to stand at room temperature for about 1 hour. Strain and serve cold.

Chillies Stuffed with Fish Paste

SERVES 4–6

225 g/8 oz white fish, minced

2 tbsp lightly beaten egg

4–6 mild large red and green chillies

1 tbsp vegetable or groundnut oil, plus extra
   for shallow frying

2 garlic cloves, finely chopped

½–1 tsp fermented black beans, rinsed and
   lightly mashed

1 tbsp light soy sauce

pinch of sugar

1 tbsp water

MARINADE

1 tsp finely chopped fresh ginger

pinch of salt

pinch of white pepper

½ tsp vegetable or groundnut oil

1. Combine all the marinade ingredients in a bowl and marinate the fish for 20 minutes. Add the egg and mix by hand to create a smooth paste.

2. To prepare the chillies, cut in half lengthways and scoop out the seeds and loose flesh. Cut into bite-sized pieces. Spread each piece of chilli with about ½ teaspoon of the fish paste.

3. In a preheated wok, heat enough oil for shallow frying and cook the chilli pieces on both sides until beginning to turn golden brown. Drain the chillies, set aside and wipe the wok clean.

4. Heat the 1 tablespoon of oil in the clean wok and stir-fry the garlic until aromatic. Stir in the black beans and mix well. Add the soy sauce and sugar and stir, then add the chilli pieces. Add the water, then cover and simmer over a low heat for 5 minutes. Serve immediately.

Crispy Crab Wontons

MAKES 24

175 g/6 oz white crabmeat, drained if canned
   and thawed if frozen, flaked
50 g/1¾ oz canned water chestnuts, drained,
   rinsed, and chopped
1 small fresh red chilli, chopped
1 spring onion, chopped
1 tbsp cornflour

1 tsp dry sherry
1 tsp light soy sauce
½ tsp lime juice
24 wonton wrappers
vegetable oil, for deep-frying
fresh chives and lime slices, to garnish

1. To make the filling, mix the crabmeat, water chestnuts, chilli, spring onion, cornflour, sherry, soy sauce and lime juice together in a bowl.

2. Spread out the wonton wrappers on a work surface and spoon an equal portion of the filling into the centre of each wonton wrapper.

3. Dampen the edges of the wonton wrappers with a little water and fold them in half to form triangles. Fold the 2 pointed ends in towards the centre, moisten with a little water to secure, then pinch together to seal.

4. Heat enough oil for deep-frying in a wok, deep-fat fryer or large heavy-based saucepan to 180–190°C/ 350–375°F, or until a cube of bread browns in 30 seconds. Deep-fry the wontons in batches for 2–3 minutes, until golden brown and crisp (if you deep-fry too many at one time, the oil temperature will drop and they will be soggy).

5. Remove the wontons with a slotted spoon, drain on kitchen paper and serve hot, garnished with chives and lime slices.

Scallops in Black Bean Sauce

SERVES 4

2 tbsp vegetable or groundnut oil

1 tsp finely chopped garlic

1 tsp finely chopped fresh ginger

1 tbsp fermented black beans, rinsed and
   lightly mashed

400 g/14 oz prepared scallops

½ tsp light soy sauce

1 tsp Chinese rice wine

1 tsp sugar

3–4 fresh red bird's-eye chillies, finely chopped

1–2 tsp chicken stock

1 tbsp finely chopped spring onion

1. Heat the oil in a preheated wok or large frying pan. Add the garlic and stir, then add the ginger and stir-fry together for about 1 minute, until fragrant. Mix in the black beans, add the scallops and stir-fry for 1 minute. Add the light soy sauce, rice wine, sugar and chillies.

2. Lower the heat and simmer for 2 minutes, then add the stock. Finally add the spring onion, stir and serve.

Baby Squid Stuffed with Pork and Mushrooms

SERVES 6–8

400 g/14 oz baby squid

4 dried Chinese mushrooms, soaked in warm water for 20 minutes

225 g/8 oz pork mince

4 canned water chestnuts, drained and finely chopped

½ tsp sesame oil

1 tsp salt

½ tsp white pepper

4 tbsp dark soy sauce and 1 red Thai chilli, chopped (optional), to serve

1. Clean the squid thoroughly, then remove and discard the tentacles. Squeeze out any excess water from the mushrooms and finely chop, discarding any tough stems.

2. Mix the mushrooms with the pork, water chestnuts, sesame oil, salt and pepper.

3. Force the stuffing into the squid, pressing firmly but leaving enough room to secure each one with a cocktail stick.

4. Line a bamboo steamer with a circle of lightly oiled greaseproof paper and replace the lid. Fill the base of a wok with enough water for steaming and place the bamboo steamer on top. Place over a medium–high heat and bring to the boil. Transfer the squid to the steamer, re-cover and steam for 15 minutes, until cooked through.

5. Using a slotted spoon, carefully transfer the squid to a serving plate. Serve with the soy sauce and chilli, if using.

Stir-fried Squid with Hot Black Bean Sauce

SERVES 4

750 g/1 lb 10 oz squid, cleaned and tentacles
   discarded

1 large red pepper, deseeded

115 g/4 oz mangetout

1 head of pak choi

1½ tbsp corn oil

1 small fresh red bird's-eye chilli, chopped

1 garlic clove, finely chopped

1 tsp grated fresh ginger

2 spring onions, chopped

SAUCE

3 tbsp black bean sauce

1 tbsp Thai fish sauce

1 tbsp rice wine or dry sherry

1 tbsp dark soy sauce

1 tsp soft light brown sugar

1 tsp cornflour

1 tbsp water

1. Cut the squid body cavities into quarters lengthways. Use the tip of a small sharp knife to score a diamond pattern into the flesh without cutting all the way through. Pat dry with kitchen paper.

2. Cut the pepper into long, thin slices. Cut the mangetout in half diagonally. Coarsely shred the pak choi.

3. To make the sauce, mix the black bean sauce, fish sauce, rice wine, soy sauce and sugar together in a bowl. Blend the cornflour with the water and stir into the the bowl. Set aside until required.

4. Heat the oil in a preheated wok or large frying pan. Add the chilli, garlic, ginger and spring onions and stir-fry for 1 minute. Add the pepper slices and stir-fry for 2 minutes.

5. Add the squid and stir-fry over a high heat for a further minute. Stir in the mangetout and pak choi and stir for a further minute or until wilted.

6. Stir in the sauce ingredients and cook, stirring constantly, for 2 minutes, or until the sauce thickens and clears. Serve immediately.

Sweet Chilli Squid

SERVES 4

2½ tbsp sesame oil
280 g/10 oz prepared squid, cut into strips
2 red peppers, deseeded and thinly sliced
3 shallots, thinly sliced
85 g/3 oz mushrooms, thinly sliced
1 tbsp dry sherry

4 tbsp light soy sauce
1 tsp sugar
1 tsp hot chilli flakes, or to taste
1 garlic clove, crushed
1 tbsp sesame seeds, toasted
freshly cooked rice, to serve

1. Heat 1 tablespoon of oil in a preheated wok or large frying pan over a medium heat. Add the squid and cook for 2 minutes. Remove from the wok and set aside.

2. Add the other tablespoon of oil to the wok and stir-fry the peppers and shallots over a medium heat for 1 minute. Add the mushrooms and stir-fry for a further 2 minutes.

3. Return the squid to the wok and add the sherry, soy sauce, sugar, chilli flakes and garlic, stirring thoroughly. Cook for a further 2 minutes.

4. Sprinkle with the toasted sesame seeds, drizzle over the remaining oil and stir. Serve on a bed of freshly cooked rice.

Stir-fried Fresh Crab with Ginger

SERVES 4

3 tbsp vegetable or groundnut oil

2 large fresh crabs, cleaned, broken into pieces, and legs cracked with a cleaver

55 g/2 oz fresh ginger, julienned

100 g/3½ oz spring onions, chopped into 5-cm/2-inch lengths

2 tbsp light soy sauce

1 tsp sugar

pinch of white pepper

1. In a preheated wok or large frying pan, heat 2 tablespoons of the oil and cook the crab over a high heat for 3–4 minutes. Remove and set aside. Wipe the wok clean.

2. In the clean wok, heat the remaining oil, then add the ginger and stir until fragrant. Add the spring onions, then stir in the crab pieces. Add the soy sauce, sugar and pepper. Cover and simmer for 1 minute, then serve immediately.

Clams in Black Bean Sauce

SERVES 4

900 g/2 lb small clams
1 tbsp vegetable or groundnut oil
1 tsp finely chopped fresh ginger
1 tsp finely chopped garlic
1 tbsp fermented black beans, rinsed and
    roughly chopped

2 tsp Chinese rice wine
1 tbsp finely chopped spring onion
1 tsp salt (optional)

1. Discard any clams with broken shells and any that refuse to close when tapped. Wash the remaining clams thoroughly and leave to soak in clean water until ready to cook.

2. In a preheated wok or large frying pan, heat the oil and stir-fry the ginger and garlic until fragrant. Add the black beans and cook for 1 minute.

3. Over a high heat, add the clams and rice wine and stir-fry for 2 minutes to mix everything together. Cover and cook for a further 3 minutes. Add the spring onion and salt, if necessary, and serve immediately.

Vegetable Dishes

Because of its vast size and varying climate, China produces an amazing variety of vegetables, and the Chinese have perfected the art of cooking them. Cooks visit the market on a daily basis to make sure they get the freshest and best vegetables available; anything even slightly sub-standard will be firmly rejected.

Vegetables are integral to every meal and are consumed in far greater amounts than meat or poultry. With very few exceptions, meat and poultry dishes are always combined with some kind of vegetable, and soups include tasty and colourful slivers. Stir-frying, in which ingredients are quickly cooked over high heat, is the usual way of cooking vegetables. The technique ensures that all-important flavour, colour and texture, as well as valuable nutrients, are preserved.

Salads as we know them in the West do not feature greatly on the Chinese menu, except perhaps in the Canton region where chefs are more inclined to try out new ideas from abroad. However, many lightly cooked vegetable dishes can be classified as salads if they are cooled and lightly tossed in a dressing.

Tofu, made from soya beans, is eaten throughout China but is particularly popular in the north where soya beans are an important crop. Hot and Sour Soup with Tofu, and Mushroom and Tofu Firepot are typical of hearty Mongolian cuisine. In regions where wheat is the staple, you'll find vegetable and noodle combinations rather than rice. Try Sweet and Sour Vegetables on Noodle Pancakes, or Chengdu Noodles in Sesame Sauce – a spicy dish from Szechuan.

Hot and Sour Soup with Tofu

SERVES 4

3 strips of lime rind

2 garlic cloves, peeled

2 slices fresh ginger

1 litre/1¾ pints chicken stock

1 tbsp vegetable oil

175 g/6 oz firm tofu, drained and cubed

200 g/7 oz dried fine egg noodles

100 g/3½ oz shiitake mushrooms, sliced

1 fresh red chilli, deseeded and sliced

4 spring onions, sliced

1 tsp light soy sauce

juice of 1 lime

1 tsp Chinese rice wine

1 tsp sesame oil

chopped fresh coriander, to garnish

1. Put the lime rind, garlic and ginger into a large saucepan with the stock and bring to the boil. Reduce the heat and simmer for 5 minutes. Remove the lime rind, garlic and ginger with a slotted spoon and discard.

2. Meanwhile, heat the vegetable oil in a large frying pan over a high heat, add the tofu and cook, turning frequently, until golden. Remove the tofu from the pan and drain on kitchen paper.

3. Add the noodles, mushrooms and chilli to the stock and simmer for 3 minutes.

4. Add the tofu, spring onions, soy sauce, lime juice, rice wine and sesame oil and briefly heat through.

5. Divide the soup among 4 warmed bowls, scatter over the coriander and serve immediately.

Mushroom and Ginger Soup

SERVES 4

15 g/½ oz dried Chinese mushrooms
1 litre/1¾ pints hot vegetable stock
125 g/4½ oz thread egg noodles
2 tsp sunflower oil
3 garlic cloves, crushed
2.5-cm/1-inch piece fresh ginger,
   finely shredded

½ tsp mushroom ketchup
1 tsp light soy sauce
125 g/4½ oz beansprouts
fresh coriander sprigs, to garnish

1. Soak the dried Chinese mushrooms for at least 30 minutes in 300 ml/10 fl oz of the hot stock. Drain the mushrooms and reserve the stock. Remove the stalks of the mushrooms and discard. Slice the caps and reserve.

2. Cook the noodles according to the instructions on the packet. Drain well, rinse under cold water, and drain again. Set aside.

3. Heat the oil in a preheated wok or large frying pan over a high heat. Add the garlic and ginger, stir and add the mushrooms. Stir over a high heat for 2 minutes.

4. Add the remaining stock with the reserved stock and bring to the boil. Add the mushroom ketchup and soy sauce. Stir in the beansprouts and cook until tender.

5. Place some noodles in each soup bowl and ladle the soup on top. Garnish with fresh coriander sprigs and serve immediately.

Classic Stir-fried Vegetables

SERVES 4

3 tbsp sesame oil

8 spring onions, chopped

1 garlic clove, crushed

1 tbsp grated fresh ginger

1 head of broccoli, cut into florets

1 orange or yellow pepper, deseeded and roughly chopped

125 g/4½ oz red cabbage, shredded

125 g/4½ oz baby corn

175 g/6 oz portobello mushrooms, thinly sliced

200 g/7 oz fresh beansprouts

250 g/9 oz canned water chestnuts, drained

4 tsp light soy sauce, or to taste

1. Heat the oil in a preheated wok or large frying pan over a high heat. Stir-fry three quarters of the chopped spring onions with the garlic and ginger for 30 seconds.

2. Add the broccoli, pepper and red cabbage and stir-fry for 1–2 minutes. Mix in the baby corn and mushrooms and stir-fry for a further 1–2 minutes.

3. Finally, add the beansprouts and water chestnuts and cook for 2 minutes. Pour in the soy sauce and stir well.

4. Serve immediately, garnished with the remaining spring onions.

Bamboo Shoots with Tofu

SERVES 4–6

3 dried Chinese mushrooms, soaked in warm
water for 20 minutes

55 g/2 oz baby pak choi

vegetable or groundnut oil, for deep-frying

450 g/1 lb firm tofu, cut into 2.5-cm/1-inch
cubes

55 g/2 oz canned bamboo shoots, rinsed and
finely sliced

1 tsp oyster sauce

1 tsp light soy sauce

1. Squeeze out any excess water from the mushrooms and slice finely, discarding any tough stems. Blanch the pak choi in a large pan of boiling water for 30 seconds. Drain and set aside.

2. Heat enough oil for deep-frying in a wok, deep-fat fryer or large heavy-based saucepan to 180–190°C/350–375°F, or until a cube of bread browns in 30 seconds. Deep-fry the tofu cubes until golden brown. Remove, drain and set aside.

3. In a preheated wok or large frying pan, heat 1 tablespoon of the oil, toss in the mushrooms and pak choi and stir. Add the tofu and bamboo shoots with the oyster and soy sauces. Heat through and serve.

Spicy Tofu

SERVES 4

250 g/9 oz firm tofu, rinsed, drained and
    cut into 1-cm/½-inch cubes
4 tbsp groundnut oil
1 tbsp grated fresh ginger
3 garlic cloves, crushed
4 spring onions, thinly sliced
1 head of broccoli, cut into florets
1 carrot, cut into batons
1 yellow pepper, deseeded and thinly sliced
250 g/9 oz shiitake mushrooms, thinly sliced
freshly cooked rice, to serve

MARINADE
5 tbsp vegetable stock
2 tsp cornflour
2 tbsp light soy sauce
1 tbsp caster sugar
pinch of chilli flakes

1. Combine all the marinade ingredients in a bowl. Add the tofu and toss well to cover in the marinade. Set aside to marinate for 20 minutes.

2. In a preheated wok or large frying pan, heat 2 tablespoons of the oil and stir-fry the tofu with its marinade until brown and crispy. Remove from the wok and set aside.

3. Heat the remaining 2 tablespoons of oil in the wok and stir-fry the ginger, garlic and spring onions for 30 seconds. Add the broccoli, carrot, yellow pepper and mushrooms and cook for 5–6 minutes. Return the tofu to the wok and stir-fry to reheat. Serve immediately with freshly cooked rice.

Mixed Vegetables with Quick-fried Basil

SERVES 4

2 tbsp vegetable or groundnut oil, plus extra
   for shallow frying
2 garlic cloves, chopped
1 onion, sliced
115 g/4 oz baby corn, cut in half diagonally
½ cucumber, peeled, halved, deseeded
   and sliced
225 g/8 oz canned water chestnuts, drained
   and rinsed
55 g/2 oz mangetout

115 g/4 oz shiitake mushrooms, halved
1 red pepper, deseeded and thinly sliced
1 tbsp soft light brown sugar
2 tbsp Thai soy sauce
1 tbsp fish sauce
1 tbsp rice vinegar
8–12 sprigs fresh Thai basil
freshly cooked rice, to serve

1. Heat the oil in a preheated wok or large frying pan and stir-fry the garlic and onion for 1–2 minutes. Add the baby corn, cucumber, water chestnuts, mangetout, mushrooms and red pepper and stir-fry for 2–3 minutes, until starting to soften.

2. Add the sugar, soy sauce, fish sauce and vinegar and gradually bring to the boil. Simmer for 1–2 minutes.

3. Meanwhile, heat enough oil for shallow frying in a wok and, when hot, add the basil sprigs. Cook for 20–30 seconds, until crisp. Remove with a slotted spoon and drain on kitchen paper.

4. Garnish the vegetable stir-fry with the crispy basil and serve immediately with freshly cooked rice.

Oyster Mushrooms and Vegetables with Peanut Chilli Sauce

SERVES 4

1 tbsp vegetable or groundnut oil
4 spring onions, finely sliced
1 carrot, cut into thin strips
1 courgette, cut into thin strips
½ head of broccoli, cut into florets
450 g/1 lb oyster mushrooms, thinly sliced

2 tbsp crunchy peanut butter
1 tsp chilli powder, or to taste
3 tbsp water
freshly cooked rice, to serve
lime wedges, to garnish

1. Heat the oil in a preheated wok or large frying pan until almost smoking. Stir-fry the spring onions for 1 minute. Add the carrot and courgette and stir-fry for another minute. Then add the broccoli and cook for one more minute. Add the broccoli and cook for a further minute.

2. Stir in the mushrooms and cook until they are soft and at least half the liquid they produce has evaporated. Add the peanut butter and stir well, then season with the chilli powder to taste. Finally add the water and cook for 1 minute.

3. Serve with freshly cooked rice and garnish with lime wedges.

Broccoli and Mangetout Stir-fry

SERVES 4

2 tbsp vegetable or groundnut oil

dash of sesame oil

1 garlic clove, finely chopped

225 g/8 oz small head of broccoli, broken
 into florets

115 g/4 oz mangetout

225 g/8 oz Chinese leaves, chopped into
 1-cm/½-inch slices

5–6 spring onions, finely chopped

½ tsp salt

2 tbsp light soy sauce

1 tbsp Chinese rice wine

1 tsp sesame seeds, lightly toasted

1. In a preheated wok or large frying pan, heat the oils, then add the garlic and stir-fry vigorously. Add all the vegetables and salt and stir-fry over a high heat, tossing rapidly, for about 3 minutes.

2. Pour in the soy sauce and rice wine and cook for a further 2 minutes. Sprinkle with the sesame seeds and serve hot.

Choi Sum in Oyster Sauce

SERVES 4–6

300 g/10½ oz choi sum

1 tbsp vegetable or groundnut oil

1 tsp finely chopped garlic

1 tbsp oyster sauce

1. Blanch the choi sum in a large saucepan of boiling water for 30 seconds. Drain and set aside.

2. In a preheated wok or deep saucepan, heat the oil and stir-fry the garlic until fragrant. Add the choi sum and toss for 1 minute. Stir in the oyster sauce and serve.

Aubergine with Red Peppers

SERVES 4

3 tbsp vegetable or groundnut oil

1 garlic clove, finely chopped

3 aubergines, halved lengthways and cut
   diagonally into 2.5-cm/1-inch pieces

1 tsp white rice vinegar

1 red pepper, deseeded and finely sliced

2 tbsp light soy sauce

1 tsp sugar

1 tbsp finely chopped coriander leaves,
   to garnish

1. Heat the oil in a preheated wok or deep saucepan. When it begins to smoke, toss in the garlic, stir-fry until fragrant, then add the aubergines. Stir-fry for 30 seconds, then add the vinegar. Reduce the heat and cook, covered, for 5 minutes, stirring from time to time.

2. When the aubergine pieces are soft, add the pepper and stir. Add the soy sauce and sugar and cook, uncovered, for 2 minutes.

3. Remove the wok from the heat and leave to rest for 2 minutes. Transfer to a serving dish, garnish with coriander and serve.

Stuffed Aubergine with Spicy Sauce

SERVES 5–6

BATTER

100 g/3½ oz besan or gram flour

55 g/2 oz plain flour

pinch of salt

1 egg, beaten

300 ml/10 fl oz very cold water

SPICY SAUCE

5-cm/2-inch piece of fresh ginger

2 large garlic cloves

2 tbsp vegetable or groundnut oil

3 tbsp chilli bean sauce

1 tsp white rice vinegar

2 tsp sugar

150 ml/5 fl oz chicken stock

STUFFING

100 g/3½ oz minced pork

½ tsp very finely chopped spring onion

½ tsp very finely chopped fresh ginger

dash of Chinese rice wine

pinch of white pepper

pinch of salt

2 large aubergines, cut into 4-cm/1½-inch slices

vegetable or groundnut oil, for deep-frying

1. To prepare the batter, sift together the flours and salt into a large bowl. Stir in the egg, then gradually add the water. Beat for at least 5 minutes, until the batter is smooth and thick. Leave to rest in the refrigerator.

2. Grate the ginger and garlic for the sauce on a nutmeg grater, discarding the fibrous parts on top of the grater and reserving the liquids that drip through.

3. To prepare the stuffing, mix together all the ingredients and set aside for 20 minutes.

4. Make a small incision (cut less than halfway through) on the side of each aubergine slice. Stuff about ½ teaspoon of the pork stuffing into the incision, smoothing the surface with a knife to remove any excess.

5. Heat enough oil for deep-frying in a wok, deep-fat fryer or large heavy-based saucepan to 180–190°C/350–375°F, or until a cube of bread browns in 30 seconds. Dip each aubergine piece into the batter and lower into the oil. Deep-fry for about 10 minutes until golden brown. Drain and arrange in a bowl or on a serving plate.

6. Heat the oil for the sauce in a preheated wok or deep pan, add the chilli bean sauce and stir for 1 minute, then reduce the heat. Stir-fry the reserved ginger and garlic juices for 1 minute, then add the vinegar and sugar and fry for 2 minutes. Finally add the stock and simmer for 2 minutes. Serve the stuffed aubergine slices with the sauce.

Sweet and Sour Vegetables on Noodle Pancakes

SERVES 4

115 g/4 oz thin rice noodles

6 eggs

4 spring onions, sliced diagonally

2½ tbsp vegetable or groundnut oil

900 g/2 lb selection of vegetables, such as carrots, baby corn, cauliflower, broccoli, mangetout, mushrooms and onions, peeled as necessary and chopped into equal-sized pieces

100 g/3½ oz canned bamboo shoots, drained

200 ml/7 fl oz ready-made sweet and sour sauce

salt and pepper

1. Soak the noodles according to the instructions on the packet. Drain well and use scissors to cut them into 7.5-cm/3-inch lengths.

2. Meanwhile, prepare the vegetables as necessary and chop into equal-size chunks.

3. Beat the eggs, then stir in the noodles, spring onions, salt and pepper. Heat a 20-cm/8-inch frying pan over a high heat. Add 1 tablespoon of the oil and swirl it around. Pour in a quarter of the egg mixture and tilt the frying pan so it covers the bottom. Lower the heat to medium and cook for 1 minute, or until the thin pancake is set. Flip it over and add a little extra oil, if necessary. Continue cooking until beginning to colour. Transfer to a plate and keep warm in a low oven while you make 3 more pancakes.

4. When you have made 4 pancakes, heat a wok or large frying pan over a high heat and add the remaining oil. Add the thickest vegetables, such as carrots, first and stir-fry for 30 seconds. Gradually add the remaining vegetables and the bamboo shoots. Stir in the sauce and stir-fry until all the vegetables are tender and the sauce is hot. Spoon the vegetables and sauce over the pancakes.

Sweet and Sour Vegetables with Cashew Nuts

SERVES 4

1 tbsp vegetable or groundnut oil

1 tsp chilli oil

2 onions, sliced

2 carrots, thinly sliced

2 courgettes, thinly sliced

115 g/4 oz head of broccoli, cut into florets

115 g/4 oz white mushrooms, sliced

115 g/4 oz small pak choi, halved

2 tbsp light brown sugar

2 tbsp light soy sauce

1 tbsp rice vinegar

55 g/2 oz cashew nuts

1. Heat the oils in a wok or large frying pan and stir-fry the onions for 1–2 minutes, until they start to soften.

2. Add the carrots, courgettes and broccoli and stir-fry for 2–3 minutes. Add the mushrooms, pak choi, sugar, soy sauce and vinegar and stir-fry for 1–2 minutes.

3. Meanwhile, dry-fry or toast the cashew nuts. Sprinkle the cashews over the stir-fry and serve immediately.

Mushroom and Tofu Firepot

SERVES 4

55 g/2 oz dried Chinese mushrooms

115 g/4 oz firm tofu, drained

2 tbsp sweet chilli sauce

2 tbsp vegetable or groundnut oil

2 large garlic cloves, chopped

1-cm/½-inch piece fresh ginger, peeled and finely chopped

1 red onion, sliced

½ tbsp Szechuan peppers, lightly crushed

55 g/2 oz canned straw mushrooms, drained weight, rinsed

1 star anise

pinch of sugar

soy sauce, to taste

115 g/4 oz dried fine rice noodles

1. Soak the mushrooms in enough boiling water to cover for 20 minutes, or until soft. Cut the tofu into bite-sized chunks, coat with the sweet chilli sauce and leave to marinate.

2. Strain the soaked mushrooms through a sieve lined with kitchen paper, reserving the soaking liquid. Heat the oil in a medium flameproof casserole or large frying pan with a lid. Add the garlic and ginger and stir them around for 30 seconds. Add the onion and peppers and keep stirring until the onion is almost tender. Add the tofu, the soaked mushrooms and the canned mushrooms and stir carefully so the tofu doesn't break up.

3. Add enough of the reserved mushroom-soaking liquid to the casserole to just cover. Stir in the star anise, sugar and several dashes of soy sauce. Bring to the boil, then reduce the heat, cover and simmer for 5 minutes. Add the noodles, re-cover and simmer for a further 5 minutes, or until the noodles are tender. The noodles should be covered with liquid, so add a little water at this point, if necessary. Use a fork or wooden spoon to stir the noodles into the other ingredients. Serve immediately.

Braised Straw Mushrooms

SERVES 4

1 tbsp vegetable or groundnut oil

1 tsp finely chopped garlic

175 g/6 oz straw mushrooms,
   washed but left whole

2 tsp fermented black beans, rinsed and
   lightly mashed

1 tsp sugar

1 tbsp light soy sauce

1 tsp dark soy sauce

1. Heat the oil in a small flameproof casserole. Fry the garlic until fragrant, then add the mushrooms
    and stir well to coat in the oil.

2. Add the beans, sugar and soy sauces, then cover, reduce the heat and simmer for about
    10 minutes, until the mushrooms are soft.

Vegetable and Coconut Curry

SERVES 4

1 onion, roughly chopped

3 garlic cloves, thinly sliced

2.5-cm/1-inch piece fresh ginger, thinly sliced

2 fresh green chillies, deseeded and finely chopped

1 tbsp vegetable oil

1 tsp ground turmeric

1 tsp ground coriander

1 tsp ground cumin

1 kg/2 lb 4 oz mixed vegetables, such as cauliflower, courgettes, potatoes, carrots and green beans, cut into chunks

200 g/7 oz coconut cream or coconut milk

salt and pepper

2 tbsp chopped fresh coriander, to garnish

freshly cooked rice, to serve

1. Put the onion, garlic, ginger and chillies in a food processor and process until almost smooth.

2. Heat the oil in a large, heavy-based saucepan over a medium–low heat, add the onion mixture and cook, stirring constantly, for 5 minutes.

3. Add the turmeric, coriander and cumin and cook, stirring frequently, for 3–4 minutes. Add the vegetables and stir to coat in the spice paste.

4. Add the coconut cream to the vegetables, cover and simmer for 30–40 minutes, until the vegetables are tender.

5. Season with salt and pepper, garnish with the coriander and serve with freshly cooked rice.

Egg Fu Yung

SERVES 4–6

2 eggs

½ tsp salt

pinch of white pepper

1 tsp butter

2 tbsp vegetable or groundnut oil

1 tsp finely chopped garlic

1 small onion, finely sliced

1 green pepper, deseeded and finely sliced

450 g/1 lb cooked rice, chilled

1 tbsp light soy sauce

1 tbsp finely chopped spring onion

140 g/5 oz fresh beansprouts

2 drops of sesame oil

1. Beat the eggs with the salt and pepper. Heat the butter in a pan and pour in the eggs. Cook for 3–4 minutes, or until set, then remove from the pan and cut into slivers.

2. In a preheated wok or deep saucepan, heat the oil and stir-fry the garlic until fragrant. Add the onion and stir-fry for 1 minute, then add the pepper and stir for a further minute. Stir in the rice and, when the grains are separated, stir in the soy sauce and cook for 1 minute.

3. Add the spring onion and egg strips, stir well and add the beansprouts and sesame oil. Stir-fry for 1 minute and serve.

Chengdu Noodles in Sesame Sauce

SERVES 4–6

400 g/14 oz fine wheat flour noodles
140 g/5 oz fresh beansprouts
1 tbsp very finely chopped spring onion
2 tbsp sesame seeds

SAUCE
1 tbsp sugar
1 tbsp sesame oil
55 g/2 oz sesame paste
1 tbsp chilli oil
2 tsp dark soy sauce
1 tbsp black rice vinegar

1. Cook the noodles according to the instructions on the packet. When cooked, rinse under cold water and set aside. Blanch the beansprouts in a large pan of boiling water for 30 seconds. Drain and set aside.

2. To prepare the sauce, beat all the ingredients together until smooth and thick.

3. To serve, toss the noodles in the sauce, stir in the beansprouts and sprinkle with the spring onion and sesame seeds.

Side Dishes and Desserts

A Chinese meal usually includes an appetizing selection of small dishes, similar to hors d'oeuvres in the West. Typical are tasty meat or vegetables parcelled in crisp-fried pastry wrappers – spring rolls or deep-fried wontons, for example. These are served with a simple dipping sauce of soy sauce, rice wine and shredded spring onion. Prawn Toasts and spicy Soy Chicken Wings are also popular. A few simple vegetable side dishes, such as Stir-fried Beansprouts or Spicy Green Beans, are also part of a typical meal.

Rice, of course, is an essential and satisfying part of most Chinese meals. Plainly steamed, it provides a complementary texture to other ingredients and absorbs the stronger flavours of well-seasoned meat and fish. Also popular, both at home and in restaurants, is Egg-fried

Rice. This dish is a good way of using up leftover rice and can easily be transformed into a filling main dish with the addition of a little meat or seafood and some vegetables.

Desserts do not feature largely in China, though at banquets or formal dinners sweet dishes are served to punctuate the long succession of savoury dishes. Fresh fruit, either on its own or as part of an impressive fruit salad, might also be served on such occasions. Irresistible Toffee Bananas and Toffee Apple Slices are popular, particularly in Beijing where chefs are adept at caramelizing sugar in hot oil. Sweet dishes are more likely to be eaten separately from meals, as between-meal snacks.

Pork and Prawn Spring Rolls

MAKES 20–25

6 dried Chinese mushrooms, soaked in warm water for 20 minutes

1 tbsp vegetable or groundnut oil, plus extra for deep-frying

225 g/8 oz pork mince

1 tsp dark soy sauce

100 g/3½ oz canned bamboo shoots, rinsed and julienned

pinch of salt

100 g/3½ oz prawns, peeled, deveined and chopped

225 g/8 oz fresh beansprouts, roughly chopped

1 tbsp finely chopped spring onions

25 spring roll wrappers

1 egg white, lightly beaten

1. Squeeze out any excess water from the mushrooms and slice finely, discarding any tough stems.

2. In a preheated wok or deep saucepan, heat the oil and stir-fry the pork until it changes colour. Add the soy sauce, bamboo shoots, mushrooms and salt. Stir over a high heat for 3 minutes.

3. Add the prawns and cook for 2 minutes, then add the beansprouts and cook for a further minute. Remove from the heat, stir in the spring onions and set aside to cool.

4. Place a tablespoon of the mixture towards the bottom of a spring roll wrapper. Roll once to secure the filling, then fold in the sides to create a 10-cm/4-inch width and continue to roll up. Seal with egg white.

5. Heat enough oil for deep-frying in a wok, deep-fat fryer, or large heavy-based saucepan to 180–190°C/350–375°F, or until a cube of bread browns in 30 seconds. Without overcrowding the pan, fry the rolls for about 5 minutes, until golden brown and crispy. Drain well on kitchen paper and serve immediately.

Vegetarian Spring Rolls

MAKES 20

6 dried Chinese mushrooms, soaked in warm
  water for 20 minutes

55 g/2 oz beanthread noodles, soaked in warm
  water for 20 minutes

2 tbsp vegetable or groundnut oil, plus extra
  for deep-frying

1 tbsp finely chopped fresh ginger

100 g/3½ oz carrot, julienned

100 g/3½ oz finely shredded cabbage

1 tbsp finely sliced spring onions

1 tbsp light soy sauce

85 g/3 oz soft tofu, cut into small cubes

½ tsp salt

pinch of white pepper

pinch of sugar

20 spring roll wrappers

1 egg white, lightly beaten

dark soy sauce, to serve

1. Squeeze out any excess water from the mushrooms and chop finely, discarding any tough stems. Drain the beanthread noodles and chop roughly.

2. In a preheated wok or deep saucepan, heat the oil, then toss in the ginger and cook until fragrant. Add the mushrooms and stir for about 2 minutes. Add the carrot, cabbage and spring onions and stir-fry for 1 minute. Add the beanthread noodles and light soy sauce and stir-fry for 1 minute. Add the tofu and cook for a further 1 minute. Season with the salt, pepper and sugar and mix well. Continue cooking for 1–2 minutes, or until the carrot is soft. Remove from the heat and allow to cool.

3. Place a tablespoon of the mixture towards the bottom of a spring roll wrapper. Roll once to secure the filling, then fold in the sides to create a 10-cm/4-inch width and continue to roll up. Seal with egg white.

4. Heat enough oil for deep-frying in a wok, deep-fat fryer or large heavy-based saucepan to 180–190°C/350–375°F, or until a cube of bread browns in 30 seconds. Without overcrowding the pan, cook the rolls in batches for about 5 minutes, or until golden brown and crispy. Serve with dark soy sauce for dipping.

Soy Chicken Wings

SERVES 3–4

250 g/9 oz chicken wings, defrosted if frozen

250 ml/9 fl oz water

1 tbsp sliced spring onion

2.5-cm/1-inch piece fresh ginger,
   cut into 4 slices

2 tbsp light soy sauce

½ tsp dark soy sauce

1 star anise

1 tsp sugar

1. Wash and dry the chicken wings. In a small saucepan, bring the water to the boil, then add the chicken, spring onion and ginger and bring back to the boil.

2. Add the remaining ingredients, then cover and simmer for 30 minutes.

3. Remove the chicken wings from any remaining liquid and serve hot.

Prawn Toasts

MAKES 16

100 g/3½ oz raw prawns, peeled and deveined
2 egg whites
2 tbsp cornflour
½ tsp sugar

pinch of salt
2 tbsp finely chopped coriander leaves
2 slices day-old white bread
vegetable or groundnut oil, for deep-frying

1. Pound the prawns to a pulp using a pestle and mortar or the base of a cleaver.

2. Mix the prawns with one of the egg whites and 1 tablespoon of the cornflour. Add the sugar and salt and stir in the coriander. Mix the remaining egg white with the remaining cornflour.

3. Remove the crusts from the bread and cut each slice into 8 triangles. Brush the top of each piece with the egg white and cornflour mixture, then add 1 teaspoon of the prawn mixture. Smooth the top.

4. Heat enough oil for deep-frying in a wok, deep-fat fryer or large heavy-based saucepan to 180–190°C/350–375°F, or until a cube of bread browns in 30 seconds. Without overcrowding the wok, cook the toasts prawn-side up for about 2 minutes. Turn and cook for a further 2 minutes, or until beginning to turn golden brown. Drain and serve warm.

Stir-fried Broccoli

SERVES 4

2 tbsp vegetable oil

2 medium heads of broccoli, cut into florets

2 tbsp light soy sauce

1 tsp cornflour

1 tbsp caster sugar

1 tsp grated fresh ginger

1 garlic clove, crushed

pinch of hot chilli flakes

1 tsp toasted sesame seeds, to garnish

1. In a preheated wok or large frying pan, heat the oil until almost smoking. Stir-fry the broccoli for 4–5 minutes.

2. In a small bowl, combine the soy sauce, cornflour, sugar, ginger, garlic and chilli flakes. Add the mixture to the broccoli. Cook over a low heat, stirring constantly, for 2–3 minutes, until the sauce thickens slightly.

3. Transfer to a serving dish, garnish with the sesame seeds and serve immediately.

Stir-fried Beansprouts

SERVES 4

1 tbsp vegetable or groundnut oil
225 g/8 oz fresh beansprouts
2 tbsp finely chopped spring onion

½ tsp salt
pinch of sugar

1. In a preheated wok or deep saucepan, heat the oil and stir-fry the beansprouts with the spring onion for about 1 minute. Add the salt and sugar and stir.

2. Remove from the heat and serve immediately.

Spicy Green Beans

SERVES 4

200 g/7 oz green beans, trimmed and cut
   diagonally into 3–4 pieces

2 tbsp vegetable or groundnut oil

4 dried chillies, cut into 2–3 pieces

½ tsp Szechuan peppers

1 garlic clove, finely sliced

6 thin slices fresh ginger

2 spring onions, white part only, cut diagonally
   into thin pieces

pinch of sea salt

1. Blanch the beans in a large pan of boiling water for 30 seconds. Drain and set aside.

2. In a preheated wok or large frying pan, heat 1 tablespoon of the oil. Over a low heat, stir-fry
   the beans for about 5 minutes, or until they are beginning to wrinkle. Remove from the wok and
   set aside.

3. Add the remaining oil to the wok and stir-fry the chillies and peppers until they are fragrant. Add
   the garlic, ginger and spring onions and stir-fry until they begin to soften. Add the beans and toss
   to mix, then add the sea salt and serve immediately.

Stir-fried Green Beans with Red Pepper

SERVES 4–6

280 g/10 oz green beans, cut into
    6-cm/2½-inch lengths
1 tbsp vegetable or groundnut oil

1 red pepper, deseeded and slivered
pinch of salt
pinch of sugar

1. Blanch the beans in a large pan of boiling water for 30 seconds. Drain and set aside.

2. In a preheated wok or large frying pan, heat the oil and stir-fry the beans for 1 minute over a high heat. Add the red pepper and stir-fry for a further minute. Sprinkle with the salt and sugar, then serve immediately.

Hot and Sour Cabbage

SERVES 4

450 g/1 lb firm white cabbage
1 tbsp vegetable or groundnut oil
10 Szechuan peppers or more, to taste
3 dried chillies, roughly chopped

½ tsp salt
1 tsp white rice vinegar
dash of sesame oil
pinch of sugar

1. To prepare the cabbage, discard the outer leaves and tough stems. Chop the cabbage into 3-cm/1¼-inch squares, breaking up the chunks. Rinse thoroughly in cold water.

2. In a preheated wok or large frying pan, heat the vegetable oil and cook the peppers until fragrant. Stir in the chillies. Throw in the cabbage, a little at a time, together with the salt and stir-fry for 2 minutes.

3. Add the vinegar, sesame oil and sugar and cook for a further minute, or until the cabbage is tender. Serve immediately.

Steamed White Rice

SERVES 3–4

225 g/8 oz rice

1. Place the rice in a sieve and wash under cold running water. Drain well.

2. Place the rice in a saucepan with just enough water to cover. Bring to the boil, cover and simmer for about 15 minutes.

3. Turn off the heat and allow the rice to continue to cook in its own steam for about 5 minutes. At this point the grains should be cooked through but not sticking together. Serve.

Egg-fried Rice

SERVES 4

2 tbsp vegetable or groundnut oil
12 oz/350 g cooked rice, chilled

1 egg, well beaten

1. Heat the oil in a preheated wok or deep saucepan and stir-fry the rice for 1 minute, breaking it down as much as possible into individual grains.

2. Quickly add the egg, stirring to coat each piece of rice. Stir until the egg is cooked and the rice, as far as possible, is in single grains. Serve immediately.

Tea-scented Eggs

SERVES 6

6 eggs

2 tbsp black tea leaves

1. Lower the eggs into the water and cook for 10 minutes. Remove the eggs from the saucepan and lightly crack the shells with the back of a spoon.

2. Bring the water back to the boil, add the tea leaves and simmer for 5 minutes. Turn off the heat. Place the eggs in the tea and leave to stand until the tea has cooled.

3. Serve the eggs whole for breakfast or as part of a meal.

Pears in Honey Syrup

SERVES 4

4 medium-ripe pears
200 ml/7 fl oz water

1 tsp sugar
1 tbsp honey

1. Peel each pear, leaving the stem intact. Wrap each one in aluminium foil and place in a saucepan with the stems resting on the side of the pan. Add enough water to cover at least half of the height of the pears. Bring to the boil and simmer for 30 minutes. Remove the pears and carefully remove the foil, reserving any juices. Set the pears aside to cool.

2. Bring the measured water to the boil. Add any pear juices, the sugar and the honey and boil for 5 minutes. Remove from the heat and leave to cool a little.

3. To serve, place each pear in a small individual dish. Pour over a little syrup and serve just warm.

Fresh Fruit Salad with Lemon Juice

SERVES 4–6

450 g/1 lb mixed melons,
   cut into balls or cubes
2 tbsp sugar

2 bananas, thickly sliced
juice of 1 lemon

1. Put the melon in a large bowl and sprinkle over the sugar.

2. Toss the banana in the lemon juice and add to the melon, then serve immediately.

Mango Pudding

SERVES 6

25 g/1 oz sago, soaked in water
   for at least 20 minutes

250 ml/9 fl oz warm water

2 tbsp sugar

1 large, ripe mango, weighing about
   280 g/10 oz

200 ml/7 fl oz whipping cream

1 tbsp powdered gelatine, dissolved in
   250 ml/9 fl oz warm water

1. Drain the sago and place in a pan with the warm water. Bring to the boil, then cook over a low heat for 10 minutes, stirring frequently, until thick. Stir in the sugar and leave to cool.

2. Peel the mango and slice off the flesh from the stone. Reserving a few slices for decoration, reduce the mango to a smooth paste in a food processor or blender. Stir in the cream and then the gelatine.

3. Add the sago to the mango mixture and mix well. Pour into 6 small bowls and chill in the refrigerator until set. Decorate with the reserved mango slices before serving.

Toffee Bananas

SERVES 4

70 g/2½ oz self-raising flour
1 egg, beaten
5 tbsp iced water
4 large, ripe bananas
3 tbsp lemon juice
2 tbsp rice flour
vegetable oil, for deep-frying

CARAMEL
115 g/4 oz caster sugar
4 tbsp iced water
2 tbsp sesame seeds

1. Sift the flour into a bowl. Make a well in the centre, add the egg and iced water and beat from the centre outwards, until combined into a smooth batter.

2. Peel the bananas and cut into 5-cm/2-inch pieces. Gently shape them into balls with your hands. Brush with lemon juice to prevent discoloration, then roll them in rice flour until coated.

3. Heat enough oil for deep-frying in a wok, deep-fat fryer or large heavy-based saucepan to 180–190°C/350–375°F, or until a cube of bread browns in 30 seconds. Coat the balls in the batter and cook in batches in the hot oil for about 2 minutes each, until golden. Lift them out and drain on kitchen paper.

4. To make the caramel, put the sugar into a small saucepan over a low heat. Add 4 tablespoons of iced water and heat, stirring, until the sugar dissolves. Simmer for 5 minutes, remove from the heat and stir in the sesame seeds. Toss the banana balls in the caramel, scoop them out and drop into a bowl of iced water to set. Lift them out and divide between individual serving bowls. Serve hot.

Banana and Coconut Fritters

SERVES 4

70 g/2½ oz plain flour
2 tbsp rice flour
1 tbsp caster sugar
1 egg, separated
150 ml/5 fl oz coconut milk
4 large bananas
sunflower oil, for deep-frying

TO SERVE
1 tsp icing sugar
1 tsp ground cinnamon
lime wedges

1. Sift the plain flour, rice flour and sugar into a bowl and make a well in the centre. Add the egg yolk and coconut milk. Beat the mixture until a smooth, thick batter forms.

2. Beat the egg white in a clean, dry bowl until stiff enough to hold soft peaks. Fold it into the batter lightly and evenly.

3. Heat enough oil for deep-frying in a wok, deep-fat fryer or large heavy-based saucepan to 180–190°C/350–375°F, or until a cube of bread browns in 30 seconds. Cut the bananas in half, crossways, then dip them quickly into the batter to coat them.

4. Drop the bananas carefully into the hot oil and deep-fry in batches for 2–3 minutes, until golden brown, turning once.

5. Drain on kitchen paper. Sprinkle with icing sugar and cinnamon and serve immediately with lime wedges for squeezing over.

Toffee Apple Slices

SERVES 6

4 apples, peeled, cored and cut into thick slices
vegetable or groundnut oil, for deep-frying

BATTER
115 g/4 oz plain flour
1 egg, beaten
125 ml/4 fl oz cold water

TOFFEE SYRUP
4 tbsp sesame oil
225 g/8 oz sugar
2 tbsp sesame seeds, toasted

1. To prepare the batter, sift the flour and stir in the egg. Slowly add the water, beating to form a smooth, thick batter. Dip the apple slices in the batter.

2. Heat enough oil for deep-frying in a wok, deep-fat fryer or large heavy-based saucepan to 180–190°C/350–375°F, or until a cube of bread browns in 30 seconds. Deep-fry the apple slices until golden brown. Drain and set aside.

3. To make the toffee syrup, heat the sesame oil in a small heavy-based pan. When it begins to smoke, add the sugar, stirring constantly, until the mixture caramelizes and turns golden. Remove from the heat, then stir in the sesame seeds and pour into a large flat saucepan.

4. Set the pan over a very low heat and place the apple slices in the syrup, turning once. When coated, dip each slice in a bowl of iced water. Serve immediately.

Almond Jelly in Ginger Sauce

SERVES 6–8

850 ml/1½ pints water
5 g/⅛ oz agar agar
225 g/8 oz sugar
125 ml/4 fl oz evaporated milk
1 tsp almond extract

GINGER SAUCE
100 g/3½ oz fresh ginger, roughly chopped
850 ml/1½ pints water
55 g/2 oz light brown sugar

1. Bring the water to the boil. Add the agar agar and stir until dissolved. Stir in the sugar.

2. Pour through a sieve into a shallow dish. Pour in the evaporated milk, stirring constantly. When slightly cooled, stir in the almond extract, then chill in the refrigerator.

3. To make the ginger sauce, boil the ginger, water and brown sugar in a covered saucepan for at least 1½ hours, or until the sauce is golden in colour. Discard the ginger.

4. With a knife, cut the almond jelly into cubes and arrange in individual bowls. Pour over a little ginger sauce, warm or cold, and serve.

Index